The Abundant Life Prevails

Religious Traditions of Saint Helena Island

Michael C. Wolfe

Baylor University Press
Waco, Texas

Library of Congress Cataloging-in-Publication Data

Wolfe, Michael C.
    The abundant life prevails : religious traditions of Saint Helena
Island / Michael C. Wolfe.
        p. cm.
    Includes bibliographical references and index.
    ISBN 0-918954-73-8 (alk. paper)
    1.   Saint Helena Island (S.C.)--Church history. 2. Penn Center of the
Sea Islands--History. 3. Saint Helena Island (S.C.)--Religion.   I.
Title.
BR555.S6 W65 2000
277.57'99--dc21

99-50591

Printed in the United States of America on acid-free paper.

Contents

Preface

Another Look at Saint Helena Island

I KNOW AN ISLAND off the South Carolina coast where the Spanish moss hangs from ancient twisted live oak trees and at night the moonlight casts eerie shadows on the narrow oyster shell roads. It is an old place. A European settlement flourished in this area long before the Jamestown or Plymouth colonies. It is a small place, only fifteen miles long and five miles wide, formed by the ocean's ferocity. Through the centuries, tidal erosion and battering hurricanes have broken the Carolina coast into these small islands separated by rivers and tidal inlets.

To reach this remote outpost one must cross the Beaufort River and then Cowen Creek. The Beaufort River spans only a thousand feet, placing the island not very far from the mainland; but culturally speaking, in the words of novelist Pat Conroy, "the water is wide" isolating the island and leaving its residents separated from the outside world.[1]

The island residents came here long ago as slaves against their will, brought from another island called Bunce, far across the Atlantic in West Africa. Even so, they love their island home on the Carolina coast. They call their island Saint Helena.

Since the early twentieth century, numerous writers have given extensive attention to Saint Helena Island, especially its unique linguistic culture called Gullah. Many have been extremely impressed by the unusual religious life of the island. However, until recently, no writer had attempted an interpretation of the religious culture as a primary goal. Margaret Creel's groundbreaking work on antebellum Sea Island religion began this exciting task, tracing the religious life of the slaves from colonial times through the Civil War.[2] But what happened to these islanders after the war?

In 1861 two religious traditions collided on Saint Helena Island. Already firmly entrenched on the island, the slaves' religion represented a mixture of Southern evangelicalism and African practices. The other, newer, tradition would be an imported faith found primarily at the Penn School established for the islanders by Northern missionaries whose Protestantism emphasized citizenship, character development, service, and self-discipline.

Saint Helena Island and the Penn School are historically important because they served as a stage on which a "rehearsal for reconstruction" transpired when the area around Beaufort, South Carolina, fell into Union army hands in November, 1861.[3] Seeking to prove to a skeptical America—North and South—that former slaves could be good, responsible citizens, Northern missionaries funded by the federal government traveled to South Carolina to labor among the newly freed African Americans.

Although the Port Royal Experiment collapsed, the Penn School survived into the twentieth century. In 1900, when the school faced financial and leadership problems, the famed Hampton Institute in Virginia began to direct the island school. Again Northern white missionaries arrived to conduct an "experiment" in educational salvation. Focusing on "character development" among the African-American islanders, the Penn School linked hands with a worldwide network of Christian organizations, progressive educators, and government agencies. Changing circumstances brought new crises to Saint Helena after World War II, and the Penn Center became one of the most important focal points of the civil rights movement. To this tiny island, time and again, Martin Luther King, Jr. retreated with his staff to hammer out their hopes for the future.

Through the years, Penn evolved into much more than a local private school. Its leaders embraced that most ancient of American Puritan dreams, "the shining city on the hill," and these missionaries came to believe that from their lonely island outpost, led and empowered by God, they could change the world. The story of the "Port Royal Experiment" and the Penn School seriously challenges the American myth of separation of church and state. Furthermore, the Penn School's history sheds enormous light on American ideals of social progressivism and the religious motivations of those ideals. Like so many other social progressives in American history, Penn's leaders were not merely building a better society, they were dreaming of the Kingdom of God on earth.

However, during the twentieth century, this American Protestant dream shifted dramatically, and the mission at Penn highlights that change. Penn's earliest missionaries arrived on Saint Helena certain that they knew all the answers to the islanders' problems. They came to build a distinctive society on the island and to proclaim a particular message: the American religion. As the years passed, however, Penn's teachers learned to listen to the islanders and to appreciate the local culture, discovering that God spoke in a variety of languages and traditions. Their story illustrates some of the continuing issues in our own day of how a larger, dominant society interacts with a smaller, local culture.

While national and even international attention focused on Saint Helena, the African-American islanders went about their own lives, practicing their own religion, and seeking God through visions and ecstatic rituals. Spiritual mothers and fathers led the churches and "pray's houses," which functioned as the absolute dominant institutions.[4] Under the cover of darkness, deep in the island woods, Christian and African traditions tightly interwove themselves as the islanders sought to discover their relationship with God and the community. In conflict and in cooperation with the beloved Penn School, the islanders did more than dream of an abstract Kingdom of God. They went about building and living in an actual community of faith, led by the voice of God who spoke to them in their visions.

The story of Saint Helena Island reveals how two vastly different traditions, missionary and islander, emerged from their own environments, how each sought particular goals for the island, and how they eventually merged into a living faith community.[5] In our present era, deeply concerned with the conflict between global and local cultures, Saint Helena is an island worth examining. As educators struggle again with the ideals of "character development," the Penn School offers many lessons, both positive and negative. Finally, in the midst of debate about the proper relations between religion and government, the history of Penn demonstrates that America society has always been cut from a seamless cloth; that religion has deeply affected our values, both public and private.

1

Antebellum Days

HILE EXPLORING NORTH AMERICA'S southeastern coastline in 1520 Francisco Gordillo of Spain discovered a large and beautiful harbor surrounded by enormous moss-draped trees. Native Americans, occupying the area as early as 8000 BC, called this land Chicora. Gordillo named the area Santa Elena. In 1526, Spanish settlers, led by Lucus Vasquez de Ayllon, and their African slaves established a colony somewhere in the vicinity, but following a slave revolt and due to starvation and fever only a few Spaniards survived to escape back to Santo Domingo. The escaped slaves integrated into local Native American tribes, thus becoming the first of the new immigrants to settle permanently in North America. During the next forty years the only Europeans passing through the area were pirates and a few Franciscans seeking to Christianize the Native Americans.[1]

During the second half of the 16th century, France and Spain struggled over the territory. In 1562, France entered the fray when explorer Jean Ribault named the region Port Royal, describing it as "one of the greatest and fayrest havens of the worlde." The French quickly established the settlement of Charlesfort at Port Royal, but when their supplies accidentally burned, the settlers abandoned the site. In 1564, under the leadership of Rene Goulaine de Laudonniere, the French planned another colony. Learning of these French incursions, Spain's King Philip II dispatched Pedro Menendez de Aviles to North America, and in September 1565, Spanish soldiers slaughtered the French colonists.[2]

Early the next year, Pedro Menendez de Aviles sailed into Port Royal Sound and established for Spain the colony of Santa Elena on the coast of present day South Carolina.   During the early years of the colony, the military garrisons of Fort San Salvador and Fort San Felipe consisted of about 330 soldiers, while nearly 200 civilian administrators, Jesuit and Franciscan missionaries, farmers, and artisans resided in the town of Santa Elena.

Working at Santa Elena, modern archaeologists have uncovered a high-status material culture, including Chinese Ming dynasty porcelain and Majolica pottery, indicating that Florida's ruling aristocratic families resided at Santa Elena while her sister city, Saint Augustine, served primarily as a military post occupied by unmarried soldiers.

By 1580, 400 civilian residents occupied the thriving town of Santa Elena. However, their survival still depended on a steady supply line from Spain, and the English and French constantly stalked these trade ships. Eventually, the colony proved impossible to protect.   In 1587, following Sir Francis Drake's destruction of Saint Augustine, the Havana government ordered Santa Elena evacuated and burned.[3]

A hundred years passed before Europeans again cast their eyes on the Port Royal islands. In August, 1684, 148 religious dissenters sailed from Scotland toward the newly established English colony of Charles Town. After a brief stop, fifty-one of these adventurers sailed farther south to Port Royal, establishing a new settlement called Stuart Town. During the next two years, Lord Cardross and Rev. William Dunlop, the leaders of the expedition, expressed high hopes in letters sent to the Lord Proprietors. However, a Spanish invasion from Saint Augustine ended their optimism. As their village burned, the colonists fled north to Edisto Island, but their descendants would play an important role in the area.[4]

Despite Spanish threats, the English still coveted beautiful Port Royal. As Charles Town prospered, the Lord Proprietors in Carolina began bestowing land grants farther south. In 1698 Thomas Nairne and John Steuart each received grants for "One Thousd Acres of Land on ye Island of Saint Helena." By 1710 the expanding Carolina colony laid plans for a new seaport at Port Royal called Beaufort.

As the coastal Carolina colony developed in the early 18th century, certain features distinguished it.   Unlike other English colonies in North America whose settlers arrived directly from Europe, Carolina emerged from the already-established English colony at Barbados in the West Indies, and its culture quickly acquired a Caribbean flavor. African slaves arrived within six months after the colony's commencement, and by 1708 Africans outnumbered Europeans in South Carolina. A Swiss traveler, Samuel Dyssli, commented that "Carolina looks more like a negro country than like a country settled by white people." By the American Revolution, blacks would outnumber whites in South Carolina almost two to one.[5]

In 1715, Port Royal experienced serious conflict with the Native Americans, and following these battles, few colonists felt eager to return to isolated Saint Helena.[6] Letters from the period tell of the hardships, the inhabitants being "mostly poor planters of corn, pease, rice . . . living at a great distance from each other." Religious and social life were almost non-existent.

In the early eighteenth century, Saint Helena's closest church lay forty miles away by water, and religious life on the island languished. The colonists at Beaufort erected the first small Anglican church in 1724, but not until the late 1730s did planters on Saint Helena Island consecrate the Anglican Chapel of Ease. It was a beautiful brick structure whose ruins still stand in a grove of pines and oaks veiled by spanish moss. However, religion still occupied few minds. Abigail Capers, a planter's wife, wrote that most people spent Sundays not in church but in amusements and in visiting friends on the island.[7]

Having little interest in their own faith, planters made even less effort to introduce their slaves to Christian doctrine. In 1739 George Whitefield, the famed evangelist, preached on Saint Helena Island and persuaded a few planters to instruct their slaves in the rudiments of Christianity. More important, in 1751 Whitefield helped in the consecration of the Euhaw Baptist Church on nearby Boyd's Creek. Descended from the earlier "Dunlop dissenters" who fled from Port Royal in 1686, this congregation returned to begin evangelization among the slaves on the various islands. Nevertheless, most planters discouraged evangelism among the slaves, fearing that the gospel would bring ideas of freedom.[8]

If Christianity was little known among Saint Helena's slaves in the eighteenth century, then what constituted their predominant religious and cultural practices? The question of how much African culture survived and under what guises has generated much debate concerning the acculturation of the slaves into the American mainstream. E. Franklin Frazier has argued adamantly that African cultural forms could not have survived the passage from Africa to America. He presented several reasons: slaves did not possess a uniform culture because they originated from diverse parts of Africa;

slaves were mixed together on slave ships and sold in the American markets without regard for tribal ties; plantations closely supervised slaves and prohibited the use of African languages; and slaveowners encouraged rapid acculturation into the plantation system.[9]

Melville Herskovits, in contrast, claimed that African religious rituals and beliefs survived well into the 20th century among African Americans, especially in the Carolina Sea Islands. Herskovits has demonstrated that Africans were not necessarily separated from their tribal companions, and that while slaves certainly came to America from throughout Africa, most arrived from West Africa's coastal areas, possessing similar cultural traits which were maintained.[10]

South Carolina's rice crop was important for maintaining African culture. By 1720, rice had become a major export and by the mid-eighteenth century, South Carolinians considered it the only commodity of any significance.[11] Carolina planters prized slaves from the West African Grain Coast, known today as Sierra Leone and Liberia, because these Africans understood rice production methods. Slave traders on Bunce Island in Sierra Leone specialized in sending slaves to coastal Carolina, and on the Atlantic's American side, major buyers such as Henry Laurens paid close attention to slaves' ethnic origins. South Carolinians' preoccupation with rice insured a greater homogeneity of slaves and enabled West Africans to transplant their culture to the Carolina coast.[12]

Evidence from coastal Carolina also indicates a common African language which survived the Atlantic passage. Lorenzo Turner's linguistic research demonstrated that the Gullah language on the islands is not a corrupt form of English (as believed by many) but rather exhibits African descent.[13] This common language base not only enabled Africans to communicate with one another, it also altered the English used by Europeans. With slaves outnumbering whites two to one, Gullah was in essence the accepted "trade language." The standard Southern dialect among both blacks and whites, especially along the coast from North Carolina to Florida, has always been a union of African and European linguistic patterns.

African cultural forms also survived because new slaves provided fresh links with the old world. Even after slave importation became illegal in 1808, island plantations received slaves directly from Africa or the Caribbean at their own docks hidden by the over-arching oaks on the dark winding tidal rivers. In the early 1860s, missionaries and army officers wrote about slaves who were "original Africans."[14] Unlike mainland plantations cut off from African influences, islands like Saint Helena periodically received "booster shots" from the old culture.

Unlike conditions on the mainland, the island plantations often went unsupervised by whites. Planters and their families avoided the malarial islands. These plantation aristocrats made their homes not on Saint Helena Island but at Beaufort or Charleston. Several planters lived in Philadelphia, Boston, or even London, and rarely visited the plantations. Supervision fell to a few white overseers but predominantly to black "drivers." Such minimal contact with American mainstream culture allowed African culture to thrive.[15]

More than mere speculation, archaeological research has uncovered material evidence indicating that African culture persisted in the Carolina Lowcountry. Prior to the 1790s, the architecture in the slave quarters clearly displayed African origins. Furthermore, when the early slaves made pottery for their own use, they modeled it after West African ceramics. Only after 1800 does a decline in African ceramic patterns and architecture indicate increased acculturation.[16]

Clearly, slaves transplanted much from their African culture to America and it thrived on the Sea Islands during the eighteenth century. In their religious life, as in other areas, most island slaves continued to practice African rituals and beliefs. Only a few heard the gospel.[17]

During the early nineteenth century, slaves began to show interest in Christianity. At the Episcopal Chapel of Ease, the Reverend David McElheran's wife had instructed island slaves in the Christian faith, but despite her efforts, she was not very successful.[18] However, the Baptists were. In 1801, the Euhaw Baptist Church, long active with slave evangelism, led a revival and established a Baptist church in the city of Beaufort. This revival proved to be a decisive moment in the religious history of the islands, as large numbers of blacks and whites converted to the Baptist faith. Out of this revival arose an institution that has fascinated and frustrated outsiders for almost two hundred years.[19]

Unknown in African-American Christianity except on the Carolina and Georgia coast, the pray's houses dominated nineteenth- and early twentieth-century religious life on the islands. Numerous scholars have made romantic connections between the pray's houses and secret African societies, but evidence indicates that the pray's houses arose as emergency measures when local Baptist churches refused to admit blacks following the revivals of the early 1800s.[20]

This fits a pattern found across the South. Relations between black and white members of the Baptist church in the South were nearly egalitarian immediately after the Revolution, when everyone worshiped together without segregated seating. However, this changed in the early nineteenth century, when large numbers of slaves were evangelized.[21] During this period, Beaufort Baptist Church rejected the recently converted local black slaves. Richard Fuller, pastor of Beaufort Baptist, encouraged his house slaves to attend services, but few other slaveholders wanted their slaves, especially the field hands, in church with them. Even Fuller made it clear that he did not desire large numbers of blacks in his church.[22]

Soon thousands of slaves desired a place for Christian worship, and yet were denied entrance into white churches. In response, slaves organized into plantation associations under the jurisdiction of the local church. Thus emerged the physical buildings known as pray's houses. Evidence suggests that the geographical region included in the Euhaw Baptist revival is the same as the island areas where pray's houses existed.[23]

Although the pray's houses emerged in the midst of revivals led by the Baptists and later by the Methodists, older African practices were transferred into the Christian rituals. White revivalists expressed particular concern about the "fatal doctrines" and the "idolatrous extravagances and superstitions . . . in the modes of worship" propagated by the "superstitious teachers." Missionaries worried about black spiritual leadership at the pray's houses:

> If it is a society, you will see a crowd of negroes, the greater part of whom must hear, as best they can, on the outside of the house. . . . But if it is only the missionary's day, you will see but very few. On the present Sabbath, we had four or five.[24]

> A black man, one of them whom they claim for their spiritual father, and, as they say, had brought them through the spirit, became corrupt and inflated with self importance . . . we fear they are rushing to ruin. . . . We have had some trouble at another preaching place, occasioned by puffing up of father S. as he is called. . . . They have appeared spell bound not to move or think without him.[25]

Despite such opposition, mission workers continued their efforts, and in 1838 another religious revival exploded along the Carolina coast.[26] As slaves flocked to the Christian faith in the early 1840s, additional pray's houses were established.

What made this revivalistic faith, taught by the Baptists and Methodists, so attractive? First, evangelical energy and vitality greatly appealed to African Americans. While Presbyterians and Episcopalians depended on catechism, Baptists and Methodists trusted in the Holy Spirit to move people. Conversion required little doctrinal understanding, only an emotional upheaval.

Second, Baptist congregational polity attracted African Americans by offering them an opportunity for independent leadership. Throughout the antebellum South, slaves found an expressive freedom within the church as independent polity allowed for greater freedom of doctrine and worship. African Americans easily established Baptist congregations since leadership was based not on any organization or education but rather on God's call. Even the illiterate could preach if called by God.[27]

One other significant element attracted slaves to evangelicalism in the late eighteenth and early nineteenth centuries. During these revivals dominated by Baptists and Methodists, the gospel of salvation in Jesus Christ combined with an emancipation message. The 1780 Methodist conference in Baltimore passed a resolution requiring all itinerant pastors to manumit their slaves and advised Methodist laity to do the same. By 1800 the Methodist annual conferences were "directed to draw up addresses for the gradual emancipation of the slaves, to the Legislatures of the States."[28]

John Leland, a prominent Baptist minister in Virginia, presented a similar resolution in 1790 to the Baptist General Committee stating:

> Slavery is a violent deprivation of the rights of nature and inconsistent with a republican government; and therefore recommend to our brethren to make use of every legal measure, to extirpate the horrid evil from the land.[29]

Did black slaves hear about such doctrines? Louis Philippe, the French prince, during his travels in the United States in 1797, wrote about the abolition seeds sown among the slaves by evangelists:

> April 5. . . . There are about 400 blacks scattered among the different farms. . . . Ideas of freedom have already made headway among them; apparently Quakers, Anabaptists, and Methodists circulate the doc-

trine . . . they [the slaves] hoped they would no longer be slaves in
ten years. . . ."[30]

The message even found its way to isolated Saint Helena where Hugh Bryan,
an island planter, preached to the island slaves, predicting they would
achieve freedom.[31]   Although such hopes and predictions proved false, and
Methodist and Baptist leaders eventually rescinded their manumission
decrees, it was within such a context that many slaves first converted to
Christianity.

By 1860 an amazing transformation had occurred. African Americans in
the South understood not merely the basics of Christianity but also its finer
points of doctrine and church policy. Southern blacks knew how to operate
their own congregations and how to pastor their own people. While African
practices survived, especially at the pray's houses, these practices took on
Christian guises and meanings. In the process of Christianization, the
African origins of the Gullah rituals were forgotten as slaves filled their
African practices with Christian meanings.[32]

It is remarkably short-sighted to suggest that no African practices
reached North America, but any defense of an explicit retention of African
religion and culture lasting late into the nineteenth century seems improba-
ble. Certainly, African cultural forms were imported and survived on the
Sea Islands in the eighteenth century, but historical and archaeological evidence demonstrates that during the early nineteenth century, African customs declined as slaves became acculturated into American society.[33]
Religiously, the slaves retained African rituals, customs, and dances, but by
the mid-nineteenth century the islanders had packed these traditions with
evangelical interpretations as they flocked to the churches to be baptized:

> The candidates came ready dressed for the waters. Every one had
> their head tied up in a Handkerchief . . . nearly all of them were
> dressed in miserable clothing. . . . After Mr. Phillips, the Minister
> had read their names and they had responded, and Old Pa Tom had
> nodded his approval to their examination, the Pastor . . . [led them]
> to the creek. Together they entered the water. . . . They immersed
> them, over one hundred and forty.[34]

Evangelicalism offered a type of freedom. Island slaves, like their poor
white co-religionists, discovered within evangelicalism the power "to come

to terms with their social existence."[35]   In the church, they found an inclusive place even though the world had excluded them. Although converted to Christianity, the slaves also converted this faith to their own culture and thus produced a rich tradition meeting their spiritual and social needs, providing themselves with a taste of freedom even before the Civil War brought emancipation.

From the beginning of the Civil War, island plantation owners felt optimistic about its outcome. In reality, South Carolinians did not understand the power of modern industrialized warfare.

Late into the evening on November 6, 1861, the citizens of Beaufort, South Carolina, and the surrounding islands speculated among themselves. For three days federal ships had gathered until forty-five steamers and gunboats waited outside the harbor. But why? Beaufort and her islands were strategically insignificant. Charleston was the important coastal target. All slept that night assured no danger existed.

However, with war enthusiasm floundering in the North, Lincoln needed an easy victory, and therefore, the Civil War's first naval battle ensued. At dawn, Commodore DuPont's sixty-gun flagship advanced into Port Royal Sound followed by his well-armed fleet. The impotent Confederate batteries opened fire. The Northern fleet easily advanced beyond the guns' range and then turned and directed a shower of shells upon the small island fortifications.

Residents on the islands awakened in a panic to the sound of the "big gun shoot." Shocked plantation owners quickly prepared for flight and their families gathered what belongings they could carry. Food remained uneaten on the tables. Family heirlooms were abandoned. Fine libraries and pianos could not be saved as "every hand was employed and every individual busied in gathering together the flats and boats from every quarter of the Island."[9] That evening, no white Southerner remained to impede the invading Union Army.[37]

When the federal troops landed, they encountered bewildered slaves left behind in the panicked flight. The Northern soldiers had rarely if ever seen black men and women. They described the slaves in their diaries as being in "the densest ignorance . . . the blackest human beings ever seen . . . bestial in appearance."[38]

Union army General Sherman faced an immediate challenge concerning the thousands of slaves and the cotton in the fields. Both were considered contrabands, captured property of war. Within a few short weeks, over

12,000 blacks poured into Port Royal fleeing toward the invading Union forces. Some soldiers offered them assistance; others sought to take advantage of the situation. One Northern officer attempted to ship blacks to Cuba for sale into slavery. The situation grew desperate, and Commodore Du Pont reported that the blacks were "almost starving and some naked or nearly so."[39]

Harvesting the cotton was the second dilemma. With the federal war fund running low, United States Secretary of Treasury Salmon P. Chase decided to replenish it by harvesting and selling the valuable Sea Island cotton. Sherman, with help from Colonel William Reynolds, used the black islanders to harvest the 1861 crop, but Reynolds's harsh methods engendered hard feelings among the islanders, and left Secretary Chase concerned about the next season's crop. Desperate to resolve these problems, Chase turned to his close friends in the American Missionary Association.

The AMA emerged in 1846 from several older Christian organizations such as the American Missionary Society (1826), the American Peace Society (1828), and the American Anti-slavery Society (1833). These early cooperative efforts among the old-line Protestant churches appeared under the fiery influence of America's Second Great Awakening when revivalists like Charles Finney emphasized justification by faith, personal sanctification, and social involvement. Two self-made millionaire brothers, Arthur and Lewis Tappan, were powerful supporters of Finney's revivals and these early Christian social endeavors. In 1840, the brothers became deeply involved with the famous "Amistad" case, when a shipload of 53 captured Africans seared the issue of slavery into the American consciousness. By 1860, the AMA had one driving concern: the abolition of slavery.

In late 1861, Salmon Chase wired Edward Pierce, a Boston lawyer and abolitionist associated with the AMA, and asked him to travel to the Carolina coast in order to inspect the situation. Pierce quickly found on arrival that he disagreed with Colonel Reynolds's methods, which hinted at graft. About a week later, Mansfield French, a Methodist minister, arrived from the AMA to discover how Northern Christians could assist the slaves. Like Pierce, French was also a close friend of the treasury secretary. French and Chase had long been involved in Christian missionary and educational work. In addition, French edited a monthly magazine entitled *The Beauty of Holiness,* proclaiming personal and social sanctification.[40]

Pierce and French soon found much in common. They both distrusted Colonel Reynolds and other army officers, and they both had tremendous faith in the ability of the black islanders to become productive, free citizens. By the time they parted company a few weeks later, they had arrived at a plan to bring missionaries to South Carolina.[41]

Thus began the Port Royal Experiment. Soon Northern missionaries sailed south filled with dreams of making the poor "savage" slaves into good Protestant Christians and productive United States citizens. Though freed from slavery, the Gullah islanders soon faced new challenges from those who wanted to "save" them and from those who wanted to take their island lands. From the swirl of these events emerged a unique culture and a religious tradition strong enough to withstand the challenges.

2

First Days Amongst the Contrabands

MARCH 3, 1862: A chilling rain fell on New York as the steamship *Atlantic* prepared to sail. Aboard the vessel, cotton agents and land speculators discussed the tremendous wartime profits available on the recently seized coast of South Carolina. Along with these entrepreneurs sailed a band of fifty-four abolitionist missionaries, twelve of whom were women. They consisted of young ministers, professors, physicians, and teachers, determined to "settle . . . the social problem of the age" by carrying the "evangel of civilization" to their enslaved black brothers and sisters.[1]

Only a month earlier, United States Secretary of Treasury Salmon Chase had approved this proposal by Edward Pierce. The mission would employ superintendents and teachers to take charge of harvesting the cotton crop and of educating the Carolina black islanders. Excited by the prospects, Northern benevolent societies had swiftly organized missionary bands to convert the "savage" slaves into good Protestant Christians and productive United States citizens. In the minds of the missionaries, these two categories were one and the same.

In many ways, the missionaries' religion could be termed the "American religion"—a Protestantism colored by an agenda of progress, patriotism, and citizenship. The missionaries' "American religion" derived from orthodox Christianity, but was predominantly activist, moralistic, and social, avoiding theology and contemplation.[2] They spoke confidently of God's work in American history. Descended from the nation's earliest Puritan traditions, advocates of the American religion actively sought to build that "shining city on the hill" which would inspire the whole world to conversion. Indeed, these young missionaries traveled to South Carolina with a single lofty goal: to convert the South into an idealized New England.

However, when the missionaries did not quickly reach their goals, and the realities of the work crushed their idealism, most lost interest in the project. Miraculously, a few struggled to remain, enduring constant hardship in order to educate the islanders. Often their mission teetered on the brink of failure but they continued to press forward, and in the end, those few who prevailed discovered a deeper faith than the "American religion."

Edward Pierce believed that a successful social "experiment" on the Carolina islands would prove all slaves worthy of freedom and capable of "useful citizenship."[3] Importing New England values to the slaves was the first goal. The islanders' lifestyle deeply disturbed Pierce and he wrote that the missionaries should concentrate on teaching cleanliness, domestic values, and the sacredness of marriage.

Second, Pierce had to insure that the "contrabands" would work the cotton fields, a need fueled both by practicality and ideology. Practically, the United States Treasury needed money to wage war against the Confederacy, and Sea Island cotton brought good prices in both Northern cities and Europe. Ideologically, Pierce needed to prove to the nation that black men and women would work without enslavement. Southern propaganda had long stated they would not, and many Northerners feared that freed blacks would be a national economic burden. The Port Royal Experiment labored to allay these fears and repudiate the propaganda.

Third, Pierce's formula for reconstruction was clearly religious. He wrote that "as part of the plan proposed, missionaries will be needed to address the religious element" and to teach a "pure and plain-spoken Christianity." Pierce required all his workers to possess "religious sentiments," attend church services, and instruct the slaves in the Bible, religious duty, and virtue.

Although Edward Pierce recognized the paternalism inherent in his plan, he did not see "paternal discipline" as an ultimate goal, intending it "for present use only, with prospect of better things in the future." He wrote, "As fast as the laborers show themselves fitted for all the privileges of citizens, they should be dismissed from the system, and allowed to find any employment they please, and where they please." Pierce conceived the experiment as a temporary strategy to aid the people "now thrown on our protection, entitled to be recognized as freemen" but as yet, not prepared to assume that role.[4]

One month prior to the missionary voyage, Pierce had arrived in Boston amid a storm of activity. His letter asking for teachers had already been published in the *Transcript*, a leading Boston newspaper, and mission societies were rapidly raising the needed funds and personnel. Some who led the push were older activists who had held abolitionist views dating back to the 1830s when an "evangelical Unitarianism," emerging from the Second Great Awakening, had worked for social change in Boston.[5] However, most were young prophets fresh from Harvard, Yale, Andover, and Brown.

Meanwhile, abolitionists in New York and Philadelphia set into motion their own plans to aid the slaves who were now being called the freedmen. Mansfield French, who had met Pierce on Saint Helena Island, recruited young zealots who had opposed slavery since 1858 when an evangelical revival had swept New York City. The American Missionary Association joined the effort and urged New Yorkers to commit themselves to this great work of God.[6] Simultaneously in Philadelphia, long-time abolitionists among the Quakers established the "Port Royal Relief Commission" to assist the freedmen.

In reality, all the talk about "freedmen" involved a leap of faith by these enthusiastic societies. In 1861, the army and the federal government did not consider the 12,000 black islanders to be freedmen, but rather "contraband," the captured property of war. Many in the North, unconcerned about black slavery, wanted only to punish the Confederacy and restore the former Union. However, the mission societies believed that the war meant much more, that God was present in this historical moment, and the "contrabands" would become "freedmen."

Despite the harsh political realities, on a cold, wet morning in early March, the first missionaries set sail with Pierce and French. Six days later as they approached land, Rev. French gathered the company for a dedication ceremony of hymns and prayer. In a sermon, Pierce emphasized the "greatness of their work" and told them that "never did a vessel bear a colony on a nobler mission, not even the *Mayflower*." He urged them to "trust in God" and that "if faithful to their trust, there would come to them the highest of all recognitions ever accorded to angels or men, in this life or the next."[7]

Who were these young missionaries? William Channing Gannett, 22 years old and a recent Harvard graduate, sailed with the first group. Gannett inherited his ideals from his father Ezra Stiles Gannett, friend and successor of the great Unitarian leader William Ellery Channing. A generation earlier, during the 1830s, Ezra Gannett utilized revivalistic methods to inspire Bostonians to labor for social change. When many found Unitarianism rather coldly intellectual, he preached a fiery religious zeal. From birth, his son William lived in this atmosphere of "evangelical Unitarianism," and in 1861 he longed to test his beliefs on the battlefield in South Carolina.[8]

Gannett's ideals were severely tested by his fellow worker, Edward S. Philbrick of Boston. Philbrick served as a superintendent over the schools and the cotton crop, and Gannett enlisted as his assistant. Philbrick started the mission with high ideals, donating a thousand dollars and traveling at his own expense. He also financially supported several mission teachers. However, within a year Philbrick would become the center of controversy over cheap land and huge cotton profits.

Charles Ware, another recent Harvard graduate, supervised the cotton crops at a plantation on Saint Helena Island. He was a member of the prestigious Ware family of Boston whose Massachusetts roots extended from the year 1642. His relatives, close friends of the Gannett family, included numerous clergy, physicians, writers, and Harvard professors. Traveling with his sister Harriet, Charles was committed to changing the islanders' lives with the American gospel.[9]

Laura Towne was born May 9, 1822, and like the other missionaries, spent her childhood among Boston's social and economic elite. While still a young woman, she moved with her father to Philadelphia where she studied medicine under Dr. Constantin Hering. She also fell under the abolitionist influence of the Reverend William H. Furness at the First Unitarian Church. His emotionally explosive sermons stirred much anxiety in Towne. When war broke out, Towne's every thought revolved around the slaves, and when the opportunity arose, she quickly joined the mission to aid them.

Ellen Murray, a Quaker and best friend to Laura Towne, arrived in South Carolina a few months later in June of 1862. Believing education to be the key to freedom, Murray immediately founded the Penn School for the black islanders and recruited Towne to teach. Towne initially resisted teaching, since she wanted to practice medicine, but within a few months she was enthusiastic about the possibilities of the Penn School.

Charlotte L. Forten, one of three African-American missionaries participating in the experiment, sailed from New York in October 1862. Forten's wealthy, crusading family had a long history as free blacks. She spent her unusual childhood in Philadelphia, where she received the finest education available, learning the gospel of abolition, women's rights, temperance, and world peace. From 1856 to 1858, she taught school in Salem, Massachusetts. Forten kept an extensive diary and her entries reveal a sensitive young woman determined to be the best at whatever she attempted. When she heard the news about the Sea Island mission, she immediately applied for a position. Hindered because the Boston missionary societies would not receive additional women at that time, she persevered, and on October 21, received a note from a friend asking if she could leave the next day with a group of Philadelphia Quakers. Forten quickly gathered her belongings.[10]

Disregarding the dangers of war and discouragement from family and friends, many young men and women set sail on the adventure of their lives. One young woman, as she waited for her ship to sail, wrote that her father did not support her decision and that, sadly, he did not even come to the dock to say good-bye. Elizabeth Botume's physician warned her not to go because the rice plantation slaves personified the "most degraded of the race . . . the connecting link between human beings and brute creatures."[11] Laura Towne's family constantly urged her to come home.

Why did young, talented and educated Northerners travel south to aid African Americans? Clearly, they sought to test their religious idealism. New Englanders influenced by the romantic movement had long cultivated a religious tradition concerning the goodness of God and the perfectibility of humanity.[12] This mission offered romantic and adventurous young Yankees the opportunity to perfect the "savages" with the American religion.

Seeking to prove themselves, some sought a "touch of martyrdom," and on the Sea Islands, they found the adventure they craved. Malaria forced William Gannett to return home briefly the first summer. Another worker, Francis Barnard, traveled to Saint Helena to serve as a superintendent and an evangelist, preaching "with more unction than any other the gospel of freedom." Friends described him as "never sad, but always buoyant." Even after malaria struck, he continued to ride about the island tending to his flock. The black islanders thronged to his funeral when he died October 18, 1862.

Samuel D. Phillips, a teacher on Saint Helena, suffered the same fate as his close friend Barnard. Already sick after Barnard's funeral, he returned to the island "feeling that the death of Barnard rendered his immediate return necessary to the comfort of his people." In the end, the islanders comforted and cared for him. On December 5, he looked up at the black faces around him, muttered the words, "Thank God," and died.

Daniel Bowe, Yale alumnus and a student at Andover Theological Seminary, preached across New England to recruit students for the mission. He then traveled south to labor among the islanders. He died of malaria on October 30. His fiancée, whom he did not live to marry, signed on as a missionary the following year and taught at the same school on Saint Helena where he had taught. Filled with the war's urgency and a longing to prove their worth, the missionaries dedicated themselves to their task. In all, seventeen died serving on the Sea Islands in the 1860s.[13]

The missionaries certainly traveled to South Carolina to prove themselves, but ultimately, these young men and women made the journey because they believed that at this particular moment in history, God was being revealed through the abolition of slavery, and they desired to participate in God's work. From their Yankee heritage and especially in the heat of war, they embraced a theology, deep in the Puritan tradition, that viewed God as working in American history through His chosen people who were obligated to carry out God's will on earth.[14]

How did the missionaries know the will of God for America? Whether evangelical or Unitarian, they all held the Bible in high regard. Evangelicals, like Mansfield French, understood the Bible as the revelation of God, but even among the Unitarians, who maintained less traditional views, the Bible provided an authoritative voice that set the norms for life. Throughout the 1850s, New England Unitarians had shown an increasing interest in scripture and church tradition, and the Sea Island missionaries of the 1860s reflected this concern. Laura Towne, originally a Unitarian but later a Quaker, made the New Testament a standard component of the reading curriculum at the Penn School, and each day students recited from the Psalms and the Ten Commandments. Believing Bibles to be a "great need" on Saint Helena, Towne and Murray joined with an evangelical society providing Bibles for every island family.[15]

Nevertheless, while scripture held a prominent place in disclosing God's will, all the missionaries believed, more than anything else, that God was being revealed through American progress. In the 1820s and 1830s, Charles Finney and other revivalists of the Second Great Awakening had implanted a social perfectionism into American evangelicalism. In addition, the romantic movement inculcated similar values into Northern culture, especially New England. Romantics understood humanity in the context of a great cosmic struggle played out on the stage of history. Involvement in this restless striving enabled one to discover meaning in life. Across the northern states, romanticism generated a political messianism dreaming of a future age of justice and freedom. In Europe and America, romanticism and social protest joined hands as writers like Victor Hugo pledged themselves and urged others to relieve the sufferings of *les miserables*. Here was their textbook, and the missionaries sailed from New York with Hugo's *Les Miserables* in their bags.[16]

Educated in a growing culture of optimism that emphasized the gospel's ethical teachings, the Yankee missionaries believed that the Kingdom of God was being revealed through American history, values, and progress. The young Yankees harbored high hopes, and their enthusiasm rose as Northern victories in the war multiplied. They felt that "with the night's close . . . [the] light dawns with a wealth of promise on a pregnant future."[17]

If God was being revealed in American history and progress, then certainly the American federal government should have a part. Late in 1863, a missionary committee stated that the island's problems "represented a question too large for anything short of government authority." In response, Congress established the Freedmen's Bureau, which worked closely with the mission societies. While the mission societies paid the teachers' salaries, the federal government provided transportation, subsistence, and housing.[18]

Eventually, the missionaries and the government's Freedmen's Bureau intermingled their efforts so much that they became indistinguishable. General Oliver Howard, commissioner of the Freedmen's Bureau and close friend to the missionaries, serves as a prime example. He had long-standing ties with the American Missionary Association and later served on its executive board from 1871-75. Howard enabled the missions to receive a wide range of federal funds for their work. In March 1867, Congress appropriated $500,000 for constructing and repairing mission schools. In 1870, Howard helped the AMA secure an additional $7500 from the bureau for the new African-American school (Hampton Institute) in Virginia. He also acquired government support for black YMCAs, which served as strong evangelical missions. Many other high-ranking officials were also connected with the mission societies. After the war, Secretary of the Treasury Salmon Chase presided over the American Freedmen's Union Commission, a private benevolent society for the former slaves.[18] Church and state smoothly intermingled in an attempt to carry forward the will of God on earth by freeing the slaves and by converting the South to a superior Northern culture.

However, for many Northerners in 1862, the war centered on the nation's unity, not slavery. Few of the federal officers and soldiers occupying Port

Royal early in the war opposed slavery. They considered the missionaries useless "nigger lovers." This uncertainty about slavery extended to the highest levels of government. On May 9, 1862, a sympathetic General Hunter proclaimed freedom for all the slaves in occupied South Carolina, Georgia, and Florida, but ten days later, fearful of political repercussions, Lincoln nullified that order.[20] The contrabands' fate truly hung in the balance as debate raged over the meaning of the war.

Fearful about the contrabands' uncertain fate, the missionaries sought to prove the islanders' worthiness by converting them to the Yankee American religion. But what did such conversion mean? In the confusion of the war years, an exact answer is difficult. Religious, economic, and political values intertwined to define this "gospel" and the meaning of conversion. One can clearly state, in contrast to the islanders' ecstatic conversions, that the Yankees believed in the kind of Christian conversion characterized by Rev. Horace Bushnell (1802-1876), a Congregational pastor in Connecticut. Bushnell represented an influential and growing stream of thought in New England which stated that a person "is to grow up as a Christian" through proper education and need never have any dramatic conversion experience. For Northern intellectuals dissatisfied by the red hot fire of revivalism, this understanding of Christian nurture came as a breath of fresh air.[21] The majority, but not all, of the missionaries who traveled to the Sea Islands held similar views, and therefore, proper education became a vital component in God's plan to convert the islanders.

With these ideals firmly in place, the missionaries specialized in building schools. Throughout the "Reconstruction" period during and after the war, northern teachers established hundreds of mission schools across the South for African Americans. Many of these eventually became prominent black colleges and universities, but the first of these schools were on the Sea Islands. They served not merely as places where students learned to read and write, but were an important context for character development and for the cultic celebration of the American religion's rituals.[22] In June 1862, Ellen Murray held her first class for nine adult students at the Oaks Plantation on Saint Helena. Soon, the Penn School, named for the Quaker William Penn, overflowed with children, and throughout the 1860s, Penn came to represent the American religion's quintessential beliefs on Saint Helena Island.

What did instructors at the Penn School teach? Naturally, they taught reading, writing, and arithmetic, but above all, the teachers sought to convert their students to civilized New England culture and character. Learning to use the right fork was as important as learning to read.[23]

Thirty years earlier, in the 1830s, such character development had served as a major component in the evangelical Unitarian schools established for the poor in Boston. The churches had provided over one hundred teachers to instruct Boston's children and adults in reading, arithmetic, sewing, and religion. Above all, they believed that contact between Boston's lower classes and the educated middle class would benefit the poor through character development. In the 1860s, the children and grandchildren of these Boston humanitarians attempted similar efforts among Carolina's freed slaves.[24]

In the Penn School's quest for character development, Yankee work ethics ranked high on the list of qualities that defined conversion. The missionaries sought to prove to the nation—North and South—that black slaves could become patriotic, civilized, productive, and self-sufficient citizens. When the sympathetic General Oliver Howard visited one school he gave them a life motto: "To try hard." This all could understand. So when he asked what he should tell their friends in the North about them, they all answered, "Tell 'em we'se goin' to try hard."[25]

Work was the favorite subject for sermons. Francis Barnard chose as his first sermon scripture text, "Work out your own salvation with fear and trembling; for it is God who worketh in you." (Philippians 2:12) Laura Towne at the Penn School wrote with satisfaction that black men and women "can and will and even like to work enough to support themselves." During the cotton harvest, William Gannett happily observed "both men and women hard at work."[26] Edward Pierce eagerly reported to Salmon Chase the children's educational achievements, pointing out that they worked hard and learned as quickly as white students. While such statements strike the modern reader as racist, these missionaries ran a race against time to create national sympathy for the slaves and to alter the war's agenda. Pierce believed that if the islanders demonstrated a conversion to Yankee ethics and self-sufficiency then "no government could ever be found base enough to turn its back on them."[27]

For proper character development, domestic values were also important to the missionaries. However, long-established island traditions presented problems. Prior to the war, South Carolina law did not recognize slave marriages, and the slaves themselves held "different opinions about the plurality of wives."[28] From the mission's beginning, Edward Pierce and his missionaries decided to remedy this situation.

Urged by the missionaries, the military authorities issued orders that "all persons living together as husband and wife should have the marriage ceremony performed, and get a certificate." The missionaries were to facilitate this mandate for a suitable wedding. Large numbers of freedmen came to the churches each Sunday to be properly wed. However, some resisted domestic conversion, and when educational methods proved insufficient, missionary Charles Ware grew impatient:

> Antony, who wanted to marry Phillis, had given her up and taken Mary Ann, without saying a word to me or any other white man. I called him . . . and told him he must go to church and be married by a minister according to law. He flatly refused. . . . I thereupon told him he must go home with me, showing him I had a pistol. . . . I gave him lodging in a dark hole under the stairs, with nothing to eat. . . . Next Sunday he appeared and was married before a whole church full of people.[29]

Proper work ethics and domestic values included the avoidance of alcohol, and throughout the 1860s, the missionaries established temperance societies. Ellen Murray presided over "The Saint Helena Band of Hope" temperance society whose 400 black members spread their gospel by every means available. Children learned temperance songs, young adults wrote original compositions, and the school staged theatrical productions. Striving to save islanders outside the Penn School circle, the teachers organized "dry" festivals during the holidays to provide entertainment. Thousands turned out for the fun, and Laura Towne rejoiced that local whiskey profits had declined.[30]

In all that they did, the missionaries labored diligently to change their world because they believed that activism and ethical behavior constituted the proof of conversion. They prayed, "We trust in God that our strength . . . be equal to our responsibilities."[31]

Such faith stood in contrast to the islanders' Christianity, where ecstatic spiritual awakenings demonstrated conversion. Activism was little emphasized, and in frustration, the missionaries wondered if any true Christians existed on the island:

> They [the islanders] go to evening meetings, stamp, shout, have the power, and get religion, and the next day fight, and swear and steal, as they did before, without apparently the slightest

recollection of last night's excitement; and at the next evening meetings, they will go through the same exercise, with precisely the same results.[32]

Naturally, the teachers found a few who met their criteria as "Christians in heart and life," and through education, the Yankees believed that the islanders would acquire a "growing appreciation of fitness and propriety." They rejoiced when young islanders "learned to ridicule the extravagant preaching, the meaningless hymns, and the noisy singing of their elders." They felt encouraged when "young people . . . [took] the matter into their own hands, formed choirs, [and] adopted the hymns and tunes of the white churches."[33]

There was the key point. In the final analysis, conversion to the American religion meant adopting the hymns and tunes and, ultimately, the cultural values of white New England. The missionaries belittled the rituals that undergirded the island culture, deeming them as "savage" and "heathen." However, the missionaries never self-consciously noticed their own rituals,[34] which were filled with the symbols of the American religion.

Ceremonial rites that flourished among the missionaries provide valuable insights into their culture and faith. July 4, 1862 saw the celebration of the first of the new holy days on the island:

> We had quite a celebration for the people on the Fourth. A stage was erected near the old Episcopal church in a cool grove of live-oaks. . . . A large flag was obtained and suspended between trees across the road—it was good to see the old flag again . . . about a thousand were present, in gala dress and mood, from all parts of the island . . . the people marched up in two processions from each direction, carrying green branches and singing. Under the flag they gave three rousing cheers. . . . It was strange and moving down here on South Carolina ground, with the old flag waving above us, to tell a thousand slaves they were freemen, that flag was theirs, that our country now meant their country.[35]

Ignoring the fact that Lincoln had not yet declared the slaves free, in faith the missionaries pushed forward with their big Independence Day celebration. Church and state united as freedom's flag waved over the Episcopal chapel, and the missionaries thrilled to see the "old flag" flying over South Carolina's heretical ground.

That November, Thanksgiving emerged as the newest holy day in the American religion. Connected with the New England Pilgrims, what could be more representative of the Yankee faith? George Washington proclaimed the first "day of thanksgiving and prayer," but the celebration only became an annual holiday under Lincoln. On Saint Helena in November 1862, Charlotte Forten heard the minister read the official Proclamation for Thanksgiving:

> You, freedmen and women, have never before had such cause for thankfulness. Your simple faith has been vindicated. The Lord has come to you, and has answered your prayers. Your chains are broken . . . put your trust in the Lord, and He will . . . guide your footsteps through the wilderness, to the promised land.[36]

A few months later, when Lincoln finally declared official emancipation in the rebel states on January 1, 1863, the missionaries discovered a holy day which exceeded all others. Thomas Wentworth Higginson, erudite New England minister and the commander of the first black army regiment in America, described the celebration rites:

> The colors were presented to us by the Rev. Mr. French, a chaplain who brought them from the donors in New York . . . just as I took and waved the flag, which now for the first time meant anything to these poor people, there suddenly arose, close beside the platform, a strong male voice, into which two women's voices instantly blended, singing as if by an impulse . . . "My Country, tis of thee, Sweet land of liberty, Of thee I sing!"
>
> I never saw anything so electric; it made all other words cheap; it seemed the choked voice of a race at last unloosed. . . . Just think of it!—the first day they had ever had a country, the first flag they had ever seen which promised them anything to their people, and here, while mere spectators stood in silence, waiting for my stupid words, these simple souls burst out.[37]

Mixing the religious and political culture, flags became a central feature in the ceremony. A church in New York had eagerly donated the flags presented to Colonel Higginson and his black regiment. Embroidered on one flag were the Biblical words of freedom, "The Year of Jubilee has come!" Reverend Mansfield French presented the flags to the colonel, and as the celebration continued into the weekend, French preached that Sunday on freedom.[38]

The freedmen quickly caught the spirit and broke into the song "My Country Tis of Thee." In the song, freedom shines a "holy light" on the land, and God is the "author of liberty," protecting it with his mighty power. For the missionaries who taught the freedmen these words, the song linked the present moment of emancipation with New England's glorious past. America was the "land of the pilgrim's pride" where "our father's God" was worshiped. Their ancestors died in the holy wars of the past defending liberty. For the missionaries, New England's traditions and history, an idealized history to be sure, constituted the true spirit of America. White Southern history only revealed a heresy broken from the authentic faith while black traditions originated from a savage and heathen African past. Salvation came only from the white North, the land of the pilgrims. Charlotte Forten described the emancipation celebration:

> Thursday, New Year's Day, 1863. The most glorious day this nation has yet seen. . . . Just as my foot touched the plank, on landing, a hand grasped mine and well known voice spoke my name. It was my dear and noble friend, Dr. Rogers. I cannot tell you how delighted I was to see the face of a friend from the north. . . . I found myself being presented to Col. Higginson. I was so much overwhelmed, that I had no reply to make. . . . I believe I mumbled something, and grinned like a simpleton, that was all. . . . I cannot give a regular chronicle of the day. It is impossible. I was in such a state of excitement. It all seemed, and seems still, like a brilliant dream. . . . The exercises commenced by a prayer from Rev. Mr. Fowler. . . . Col. H[igginson] introduced Dr. Brisbane. . . . He read the President's Proclamation, which was warmly cheered. Then the beautiful flags presented by Dr. Cheever's church were presented . . . by Rev. Mr. French. Immediately at the conclusion, some of the colored people—of their own accord sang "My Country Tis of Thee.". . . Ah, what a grand, glorious day this has been. The dawn of freedom which it heralds may not break upon us at once; but it will surely come, and sooner, I believe, than we have ever dared hoped before.[39]

The black islanders certainly interpreted these events in religious, ritual-istic terms because the rites in this new Yankee religion carried power to con-vert slaves into freedmen. On January 1, 1863, old men walked for miles and mothers brought their infants to receive the benediction of the Proclamation because they feared that anyone not present to hear the ritual words would be left in slavery. They referred to Abraham Lincoln as "Pa Linkum" in the same way that they addressed their pastors who led them in conversion at the pray's houses. Following Lincoln's death, one islander told Laura Towne, "Lincoln died for we, Christ died for we, and me believe him de same man."[40]

Rituals also flourished at the Penn School. Throughout the United States, the school system has always served as a particularly important context for American cultic celebration.[41] Penn's ceremonies imparted importance to the school, encouraging the islanders to respect and value education, the cor-nerstone in the American religion.

Each June, the Penn School conducted closing exercises, "the great event of the year," at the Brick Baptist Church. Proud former students flocked back to keep in contact with the school and the ideals taught there. Young stu-dents sang, recited poetry, and read speeches. Ellen Murray directed dra-matic performances to educate the crowd, while Towne conducted temper-ance programs.

During these closing exercises, the building's decor and the students' attire provided visitors with a visual demonstration of the faith taught at the Penn School. The teachers and students decorated the church with flags showing their patriotism. The children dressed in "good taste" and their recitations taught "a splendid lesson for them and for all the island." Songs and skits emphasized the importance of a clean home, good character, and self-sufficiency through hard work.[42]

Such rituals helped catechize the black islanders into the new creed, but a wide gap still existed between the missionary religion and the islanders' faith. Under the cover of darkness, the islanders celebrated and worshiped in their own fashion, which for the missionaries represented a religious antithesis:

> Then began one of those scenes, which, when read of, seem the exaggerations of a disordered imagination; and when wit-nessed, leave an impression like the memory of some horrid nightmare—so wild is the torrent of excitement, that, sweeping

away reason and sense, tosses men and women upon its waves, mingling the words of religion with the howlings of wild beasts, and the ravings of madmen.[43]

Clearly, progress required much time and effort, perhaps more than the Yankees had anticipated, but the Kingdom of God would come and it would look like New England. The missionaries wrote:

> New England can furnish teachers enough to make a New England out of the whole South, and, God helping, we will not pause in our work.
>
> Man thinks two hundred years is a long time . . . but it is only as a week to God, and in his own time—I know I shall not live to see the day, but it will come—the South will be like the North— . . . God is just.[44]

When rapid cultural conversion did not occur, most of the missionaries turned their thoughts toward home, but a few discovered a deeper faith in the midst of their wartime suffering. When they first arrived directly from the finest cultural and educational centers of the North, the missionaries victoriously and paternalistically thought they knew all the answers to the islanders' problem. This initial optimism and then later disappointment is the true significance of the Port Royal Experiment. The missionaries' experience foreshadowed the confusions and contradictions of the post-war reconstruction efforts. Lessons could have been learned from this "rehearsal" on the islands, but they were not, and in the end, the North turned its back on the South.[45]

Several problems drove the Yankees home: conflict with the military; temptations of wealth; theological conflict; and loss of Northern idealism. The missionaries went to the Sea Islands searching for "peace and zeal . . . a band of fellow workers living in harmony with combined effort." Instead, they found "friction in every quarter—military, religious, and political."[46]

Problems with the federal military struck the missionaries almost immediately. Their very presence implied that the army had inadequately handled the contrabands. Furthermore, early in the war many Northern officers and enlisted persons did not support abolition. They fought to punish the South for breaking with the Union, not to free the slaves. While sailing to South Carolina, Laura Towne met a Colonel Morrow who told her that "if we are fighting for slavery abolition," he would "obey Lincoln's orders, but curse him in his heart." The enlisted personnel felt much the same. A young Union soldier wrote to his mother in Massachusetts: "Everything here . . . has been sacrificed to . . . the misplaced philanthropy of Edward L. Pierce. . . . Philanthropy is a nuisance in time of war. . . . I respect the missionaries . . . but they have no business here."[47]

Early in the effort, Pierce came into sharp conflict with the military authorities. Two months after the missionaries' arrival, when Pierce questioned Colonel William H. Nobles about his methods for handling the cotton, Nobles reacted violently, beating Pierce badly before soldiers could break them up. Nevertheless, Pierce refused to retreat. He consistently voiced complaints against the Union army and always feared that after the war the government agents would recommend turning the black islanders back over to their former masters. Pierce was determined that history would take a different course.[48]

Almost all the teachers and superintendents stationed near the military camps came into conflict with the army. Both Harriet Ware and Laura Towne wrote to friends about the mistreatment of the islanders:

> The New York regiment . . . were landed on this island, and they are doing all sorts of mischief. They take the people's chickens, shoot and carry off their pigs, and when the people defend their property, they shoot the men and insult the women. They have burned a row of houses near Lands End, because, when stealing a man's pigs, he fired upon them from his window.[49]

Eventually, serious conflict arose over the drafting of black soldiers. On May 11, 1862, General Hunter commanded Pierce to send every able-bodied man to Hilton Head Island. That evening the missionaries sat anxiously brooding over their hot tea, talking in low depressed tones. Feeling distraught, Harriet Ware and Laura Towne walked to a nearby pray's house for quiet prayer.

The next day, Union soldiers came for the black men. Towne and Ware were working when the soldiers ordered the islanders to accompany them. Ware spoke up saying that she knew nothing concerning such proceedings, but then encouraged the men to cooperate since two soldiers stood conspicuously brandishing weapons. Towne wrote:

It made my blood boil to see such arbitrary proceedings, and I ached to think of the wives, who began to collect in the little street, and stood looking towards their husbands and sons going away so suddenly.

The Union army seized about four hundred men for the camp at Hilton Head, but other black men did what they had done for two hundred years when trouble struck: they escaped into the forest. By nightfall, the troops began hunting them down. At midnight, Towne knocked at several doors to check on the women but even the women and children had fled. Towne learned later that, "They kept watch along the creek all night . . . trembling with fear." An old lame women, Aunt Bess, could not run when her family went into the woods. The next day she pleaded with Laura Towne: "Oh, you be quick and cure me, missus,—dey kill me,—dey kill me sure—lick me to death if dey comes back. Do get my foot well so I can run away."[50]

The second area of conflict for the missionaries concerned land purchases. During their first year in South Carolina, many of the teachers caught "land fever," and decided to help themselves while assisting the islanders. The previous August, Congress had levied a $20,000,000 yearly tax on all states, including the insurrectionary states, in order to wage the war. In the rebel states where the military had seized territory, tax commissioners sold land for the non-payment of taxes. In South Carolina, agents ordered the first land sales for February 11, 1863 and included the Port Royal islands and the entire town of Beaufort.

Laura Towne and a few others protested the rapid land sales since they wanted land reserved for African Americans. Towne urged her opinions on Generals Saxton and Hunter, and "Saxton caught at the idea."[51] While Towne and Murray cheered, other missionaries raged against the interference. Edward Philbrick, a head superintendent, demanded immediate sales claiming he wanted to buy land to save it from outside speculators who would cheat the islanders. Writing to friends, he stated:

> I . . . don't undertake it for the sake of making money at all, but for the sake of carrying out to a more satisfactory issue the present short lived and unfairly judged experiment of free labor, and for the sake of keeping the people out of the hands of bad men.[52]

In March 1863, the War Department placed pressure on General Saxton and forced the land sales. However, Saxton still restricted the sales and arranged for the United States government to purchase two-thirds of the property at an average cost of 34 cents per acre. The teachers and superintendents bought the remaining third at about one dollar per acre. Philbrick, with financial backing from investors in Boston, procured 6,795 acres valued by the tax commissioners at $24,000. He paid only $7,000 for nine plantations on Saint Helena Island and two plantations on Ladies and Morgan islands.

For the next two years, Philbrick operated a private social experiment aided by teachers and superintendents already on Saint Helena. Among them was the idealistic William Gannett. Although sincere in his beliefs, when the 1863 harvest arrived he felt embarrassed at his "ridiculously large" income. By February 1864, he wrote to his father, Rev. Ezra Stiles Gannett:

> Did you know we had long ceased to be . . . Gideonites? We are nothing now but speculators, and the righteous rail against us. . . . You cannot know how amusing it is to see in our letters of this time any words about "philanthropy," "noble mission" "glorious work" &c. . . . We are only speculators now,—we are making money out of the negros' ill paid labor. We have but little reputation except for prosperous selfishness.

Philbrick consistently maintained that as soon as the black islanders "matured," he would sell the land to them at cost. However, in 1865, when Philbrick sold the real estate, white Northerners obtained the lion's share with only small tracts being sold to black islanders. He received between $5 and $10 per acre for the plantations he had acquired two years earlier for one dollar per acre.[53]

The land sales generated tremendous conflict among the missionaries. Encouraging African Americans to purchase land themselves, Towne explicitly warned them "against trusting to Mr. Philbrick to buy for [them.]" Methodist minister Mansfield French preached to the islanders, declaring that men like Philbrick "were getting rich by the labor of the blacks . . . lining their pockets, [but] their laborers were no richer at the end of the year than they were at the beginning." French urged the islanders "to plant for themselves rather than for others."[54]

In addition to the military problems and the land conflicts, religious differences divided the missionaries. Since the 1830s, religion had split the abolitionist camp. The New York movement emerged from Midwestern evangelical revivals, while Boston abolitionists had their earliest roots in the soil of transcendentalism and Unitarianism. The missionaries on Saint Helena in the 1860s divided along these same lines. Mansfield French, an evangelical Methodist minister friendly to the excited rituals of African-American Christianity, wrote Treasury Secretary Salmon Chase that "the Unitarians don't get hold of things in the right way, for the people are mostly Baptist, and like emotional religion better than rational." Meanwhile, religious enthusiasm among the evangelical New Yorkers embarrassed the Boston Unitarians. They criticized French saying, "Mr. French . . . is . . . appealing too much to the Religious sentiment of the people and not aiming sufficiently to strengthen them in principle and purpose."[55]

The two groups also divided over the question of assistance to the freedmen. The evangelicals believed that the islanders needed and deserved full assistance from the missionaries and the government. French wrote, "God's programme involves freedom in the largest sense—Free soil, free schools, free ballot boxes, free representation in state and nation. . . . the people need . . . teachers, helpers, men who . . . are not ashamed to bear the cross of the black man." Edward Philbrick and many among the Boston Unitarians disagreed. They thought that excessive assistance would prove harmful by making the islanders dependent. The islanders should work for their freedom.[56]

The Philadelphia contingent, financially backed by Quakers, sought to provide a middle ground between the New Yorkers and the Bostonians. Although originally a Unitarian, Laura Towne proved highly ecumenical while working under the auspices of the Quaker Relief Committee, and she eventually converted to the Quaker faith. Open to the evangelical faith, Towne taught Sunday School at the Baptist church, distributed Bibles for the American Bible Society, made the Bible a central component in a Penn School education, and led music from the evangelical Moody-Sankey hymnal. At the same time, while she believed that ministers should teach Bible doctrine, she also demanded that some "good sense" be taught.[57]

During the war years, most of the missionaries were filled with enthusiasm, overlooked their differences, and preserved an ecumenical spirit. However, when the national conflict ended, few common goals still existed, and the Boston and New York bands drifted apart. In 1866, two plans emerged to unite the societies. The American Missionary Association (AMA) led the evangelical effort and the Unitarians founded the American Freedmen's Union Commission (AFUC). Initially, the two groups attempted to maintain communion, and evangelicals even occupied positions with the AFUC. However, their differences exploded when the AFUC suddenly told the teachers that the Commission considered them "not missionaries, nor preachers, nor exhorters" and that they should have "nothing to do with churches, creeds, or sacraments." Evangelicals defected and quickly joined the AMA which sustained African-American schools in the South well into the twentieth century. The AFUC disbanded in 1869.[58]

As tension mounted among the workers, only the Yankee dream of educational enlightenment for the freedmen remained. But harsh reality dashed even those ideals. Disillusionment arose at the schools as the islanders' slow progress disappointed visitors connected with the mission societies. Elizabeth Botume, teaching on the islands, wrote:

> One [visiting] gentleman asked, "How do these children progress in arithmetic? . . . Are any of them able to take up book-keeping?"
>
> At first I thought he could not be in earnest, but he looked so grave, I replied only a few were able to count to one hundred.

The teachers worked ever harder and Botume drilled her class relentlessly prior to another visiting group's arrival. However everyone froze when one man asked, "Children, who is Jesus Christ?" Suddenly there came an answer: "General Saxby, sar." Upon this an older boy sprang up and . . . exclaimed, "Not so, boy! Him's Massa Linkum."[59]

In the end, Unitarian George Stetson wrote in *The Unitarian Review*, "The negro, as a polemic or social subject, is become somewhat tiresome. . . . He is no longer of any interest to the public."[60] With such sentiments, the missionaries drifted home heartbroken and unsure if their work had accomplished good or evil. John Hunn, a Quaker who worked with the "underground railroad" prior to the war, left the islands complaining about the laziness of the islanders. Charles Ware, a young Harvard idealist when he arrived in 1862, wrote at the end of the war: "It is certain their freedom has been too easy for them, they have not had a hard enough time of it. In many cases they have been fair spoiled."[61]

Edward Pierce left the mission early. As the primary leader, he had suffered much abuse from the military. On his last Sunday he spoke at the Brick Baptist Church weeping as the black crowd mobbed him seeking a final touch from the man who had come to set them free. Pierce was later offered the appointment as South Carolina's governor of reconstruction but, disappointed with the experiment's outcome, he declined the position.

William Gannett left the Sea Islands in 1865 and returned to the ministry. Throughout his life, he helped support the Penn School financially with a $350 yearly gift.[62]

Rev. Mansfield French remained on the islands until 1872. Popular with the islanders, in 1868 he ran for the United States Senate on the South Carolina Republican ticket but was forced to withdraw his bid after being attacked by the *New York Times*. Accusations concerning land profits proved to be false but the stories ended his political career before it even started.[63]

Elizabeth Botume remained on Saint Helena for two decades. Laura Towne and Ellen Murray never left the Penn School. Towne's brother died in 1875, leaving her money which she invested entirely in the school. Two years later, Ellen Murray received an inheritance which she likewise used for the school. Thereafter, living from their own funds, neither accepted a salary for their work at Penn.[64]

Why did these women remain on Saint Helena Island after all the others left? They discovered on the islands a life work, and even more important, a deeper faith and a new humility. The missionaries all arrived in South Carolina confident that they could solve the "social problem of the age." However, those few who endured the long years discovered that the American religion's triumphant vision was inadequate. Humbled by the horrors of the war and with their old victorious confidence shaken, they discovered how little they really knew about God and humanity, especially in the midst of suffering. Ellen Murray recalled:

> A sick woman came to me one day. . . . After listening to her story . . . I said, "Auntie, that is beyond me. I really do not know what to do for you."
>
> . . . "O, missis! You'na can read books, an' in course you knows more'na we."
>
> Yes, I could read books, but they did not tell me everything. In fact, . . . I discovered they told me very little of what I needed to know most."

Another day, a black woman petitioned Elizabeth Botume to help a young, pregnant girl on the island, but Botume firmly decided that she would not help this sinful girl:

I have said I would do nothing for that girl, and I must keep my
word.
She dropped her head, and said very slowly,—
"That's so, ma'am. You knows best. You mus' be right, fur you'-
na kin read the Bible, an' so you mus' know best . . . and what
does the Bible teach me? Let him that is without fault cast the
first stone."
I sprang up and called her back. It seemed . . . I could not work
fast enough making up the bundle of clothing and groceries. . . .
All day her words were in my mind. "You mus' know best."
What did I know, that I should sit in judgement? Absolutely
nothing.[65]

Prior to the Civil War, the American civil religion, emerging from the
American Revolution, centered only on themes of victory and progress. The
early missionaries certainly arrived on the Sea Islands with that spirit, and
throughout the war many never grew beyond it. On April 14th, 1865, a great
Northern victory celebration was held in Charleston, South Carolina All the
missionaries attended to hear speakers like the great abolitionist William
Lloyd Garrison and famed Northern preacher Henry Ward Beecher.
During his speech, Beecher victoriously and optimistically proclaimed,
"Reconstruction is easy" if only we will all believe in "one nation, under one
government, without slavery." If only. That day Laura Towne expressed
doubts in her diary, and that night her doubts proved true at Ford's Theater
in Washington, D. C. when President Lincoln was assassinated. The war
brought a new national self-understanding, embracing both victory and suffering, life and death.[66] Those teachers who remained on the islands after the
war embraced that suffering spirit and discovered a new faith beyond the
victorious American religion.

Throughout the late nineteenth century, Towne and Murray poured
themselves out on the altar of the Penn School where they instructed about
200 students annually. Furthermore, by serving on the county public board
for black schools, Towne stocked regional classrooms with Penn graduates
as teachers, thus expanding her influence. Though surrounded by violence
and struggle, and disappointed with corruptions in the radical reconstruction government, Towne and Murray never abandoned their mission. They
labored year after year to maintain land ownership and a quality education
for the islanders, never losing faith in the freed African Americans. At the

f the century, as Towne journeyed back to Saint Helena after a visit to
lelphia, she talked with a man on the train. To the very end, she
ned the fiery old missionary:

> He said the whole race of niggers ought to be swept away, and I
> told him my business was with that race and that they would
> never be swept away, so he was disgusted and went away, leav-
> ing me to read in peace.[67]

3

The Islanders, 1861–1900

(VOICE OF BIG PA, Saint Helena resident) In my own land I was the son of a big chief . . . but the Lord say, "No, I got something better in store. . . . You goin' to be my servant. . . . I might have been a heathen chief . . . but now I'se a servant of God, which is much higher, slave though I be."

(Big Pa's son) One day Big Pa hear that Massa Lincoln sent down a paper . . . to say we'se all free! . . . All the people . . . get up 'fore day clean [sunrise] an' take the babies in their arms, 'cause they did not want the little ones lef' out of freedom. . . .

Big Pa been too old an' feeble to walk all that way [but] . . . "Son," he say, "I was born free an' I'se goin' to die free. Bring me my stick, 'cause we'se goin' to get our freedom."

. . . When we done arrive, a man been readin' the paper. . . . I couldn' get the understandin' of it, but Big Pa, he look like he could go on listenin' until Judgement Day. . . . When the man finish' readin' the paper . . . Big Pa lose all his strength . . . an' fall where he stood. They carry him away from the crowd an' . . . he lie so quiet I think he must be dead, when of a sudden he open his eyes an' say, ". . . go tell the Colonel please I must for see him before I die."

When the Colonel come, he say, "Colonel, is you plum sure I is a free man?" . . . the Colonel say, "You are as free a man as I am this day."

"Thank the Lord, I born free an' die free!" Then he just smile' an' shut his eyes.[1]

Rarely in history does a single day's events bring such dramatic change, but in Saint Helena Island's case, November 7, 1861, stands as a watershed. That afternoon the slaves loaded supplies on boats as their white owners prepared to flee from the approaching federal troops. Watching the boats sail away from the island, the slaves unknowingly bid good-bye to their former life. By January 1, 1863, with the Emancipation Proclamation read, freedom's new day had fully dawned. With missionary aid, the islanders acquired significant land ownership, a solid educational foundation, and increasing economic opportunities. Without question, Saint Helena's residents fared better than most African Americans.

But the late nineteenth century brought the islanders numerous crises that threatened their existence, both economically and culturally. Former plantation owners wanted their land back. Yankee investors coveted the property. The missionaries wanted to eradicate the island's "heathen" culture. And periodically, the ocean raged across the island.

Nevertheless, concerning the land, their religious culture, and the very fabric of their lives, the islanders held on to much because they adapted to the future while maintaining the past. In the same manner that they had earlier embraced evangelical Christianity without losing African traditions, late-nineteenth-century islanders incorporated new values into their lives without relinquishing their old faith.

Saint Helena's population soared during the Civil War. As the conflict shattered the Southern states, countless black refugees fled toward the Sea Islands, seeking aid from the Northern invaders. Even after the war, many African Americans remained, seeing the isolated islands as a unique opportunity to escape white oppression.[2]

Prior to the Civil War, Nancy Singleton worked as a slave near Greenville, North Carolina. All her life she dreamed of freedom but when the war ended, emancipation brought the "starving time." Nancy heard rumors of islands where freedmen could purchase land, and, with great determination, she embarked on the adventure of her life. Traveling with a handful of other freed slaves, she cut her hair short so as to be less recognizable as a woman, acquired a leaky boat, and sailed through the outer banks of North Carolina, past Cape Fear, and into South Carolina waters. Along the way, the boat began to leak in earnest and she tore her coat and stuffed the rags into the holes. The resolute group sailed past islands such as Pawleys, Johns, and Seabrook before turning beyond Edisto Island into Saint Helena Sound.

There on Saint Helena, around 1867, she purchased eight acres of marsh-front property on Village Creek for fifteen dollars an acre. Just five years ear-lier, Yankees like Edward Philbrick bought island property for only a dollar an acre. Nevertheless, Nancy was thrilled to acquire the acreage and swore that her family would never lose the land. She told them, "Never sell the land. Okay to move to the city, work or live in the city but never sell. When you have no job or food, you can always come here to farm and fish."[3]

Separated from the mainland by the wide Beaufort River and surround-ed by endless creeks and swamps, the island provided escape for many African Americans, like Nancy Singleton, weary of white control. On the island they could build their own society and cultivate their own traditions, including a unique religious culture.[4]

Alongside the churches in the late 1800s, a colorful local folklore flour-ished on the island. Laura Towne wrote concerning a man who suspected an old woman named "Mom Charlotte" of witchcraft. He believed that each night she "hagged" the islanders, leaving her body in order to ride her sleep-ing victims, thus causing horrible nightmares. In November 1867, the man broke into Charlotte's house and nearly beat her to death, believing that she had cursed him. The next day, Towne cared for the battered woman and tried to convince the man that his beliefs were false. He felt bad about hurting Charlotte, but remained convinced that he needed to protect himself against the hag.

Much coverage has been given to this fascinating island folklore with its African roots, but following the Civil War the predominant religious tradi-tion on Saint Helena was evangelical Christianity. While African customs continued to provide much ritual, Christian theology informed those rites. By 1860 virtually all conscious memory of the African rituals' original mean-ing had eroded.[5] Therefore, scholarship that ignores Christianity cannot hope to understand the life of the Gullah islanders.

Preachers, even if illiterate, memorized large portions of scripture and filled their long sermons with Biblical passages. Many sermons seemed a mosaic of endless passages as island ministers creatively linked scattered quotations and allusions into a cohesive whole. They filled their prayers with quotations from the Bible, making them among the most creative forms of Gullah oratory. Prayers were based on a set tradition of rhetorical skills. Both men and women prayed during worship, sometimes as long as twen-ty-five minutes without pausing.

Believers considered such abilities a gift from God, and this gift was passed down through certain formulaic expressions. Sea Island prayers began with a quotation from the Bible, often from the Lord's Prayer. Missionary Elizabeth Botume reported prayers that repeated scripture passages heard in a just-delivered sermon. Following the Biblical quotes, personal petitions commenced, but they were still laced with Biblical references.

> Master, could I come this evening excepting my knees are down at the floor? . . . Father, we down here this evening, Heavenly Father, asking for your mercy. . . . Hallowed be thy name, They kingdom come, Oh Lord. Let thy holy and righteous will be done on this earth.[6]

These alliterations, repetitious phrases, and allusions created a rhythmic incantation. Meanwhile, the congregation maintained the leader's established rhythm through verbal responses, foot tapping, or swaying motions. While informed by the Bible, these invocations follow West African prayer styles, which use strong rhythm and chanted delivery. Researchers have suggested that many congregation members simply responded to the rhythmic chant without understanding the prayer or sermon content. However, the extensive scripture memorization used in sermons and prayers indicates that many worshipers paid attention to the words, not merely the rhythm.[7]

In fact, scripture filled the daily conversation on Saint Helena. Literate islanders read to their friends from the Bible, as seen one morning when one missionary discovered a "knot of young men seated there [by the road], with one of their number reading to the rest from the Testament." Botume reported that the islanders "had profound respect for quotations from the Bible." When a problem emerged, islanders sought a direct answer from the Word. Sometimes this practice presented difficulties when no direct word could be found. In one case, a woman desired to marry a second husband after her first had been missing for several years. The woman begged missionary Botume to intercede for her. Botume met with the local minister and a church elder but the whole issue revolved around one question asked by the elder: "Do you ever read your Bible? If you do, tell me if you ever found anything in it to fit such a case as this."[8]

Most important, islanders understood the scriptures primarily as a revelation of Christ. In sermons, prayers, and conversation, Gullah biblical interest centered on Christ's suffering, crucifixion, and resurrection. Whatever hardships they experienced, the islanders always emphasized that

Jesus had suffered more for them. When a woman found herself separated from her husband, she cried out and believed that Jesus appeared to her:

> You say you're parted from your husband? You're not parted from your husband. You're jest over a little slash of water. Suppose you had to undergo what I had to. I was nailed to the Cross of Mount Calvary. And I am here today. Who do you put your trust in?

Gullah islanders, like most Southern Protestants, ignored much doctrinal teaching. Instead they emphasized the cross, each Sunday urging sinners toward repentance and salvation in Christ.[9]

Music, perhaps more than any other means, communicated the Biblical message to Saint Helena islanders, allowing the illiterate to memorize large portions from scripture. Thomas Higginson, commander of the first black regiment in the Sea Islands, commented that "almost all their songs were thoroughly religious," filled with phrases concerning the Jordan River, the dying Lamb, bearing the cross, and the Bible as the way to God.

> Oh, what ship is that you are sailing aboard?
> 'Tis the old ship o' Zion, hal-le-loo!
> Oh, what is the compass you've got aboard the ship?
> The Bible is our compass, hal-le-loo!
> Oh, the Bible is our compass, halleloo![10]

Gullah music also formed the foundation for the ecstatic rituals whereby islanders sought a divine revelation. Black spirituals have often been studied simply as a musical form, but the songs cannot be understood appropriately apart from their ritual context in the "shout." Only when the music and dance rituals are viewed as a whole can one fully appreciate their significance.

> The true shout takes place on Sundays or on praise nights through the week. . . . more than half the population of the plantation is gathered together. . . . The benches are pushed back to the wall when the formal meeting is over, and old and young, men and women . . . all stand up in the middle of the floor, and when the "sperichil" is struck up, begin first walking and by-

and-by shuffling round, one after the other, in a ring. The foot is hardly taken from the floor, and the progression is mainly due to a jerking, hitching motion, which agitates the entire shouter, and soon brings out streams of perspiration. . . . Song and dance are alike extremely energetic, and often, when the shout lasts into the middle of the night, the monotonous thud, thud of the feet prevents sleep within half a mile of the praise-house.[11]

As early as 1862, observers like Laura Towne instinctively felt that the shout and ring dance preserved ancient African rituals. Modern work in Africa has documented the same circular dancing where the feet do not leave the ground and where the dancers' motor behavior appears very similar to that found in island worship services. For example, during the shout, Sea Island worshipers occasionally waved a handkerchief, a movement also performed in West Africa to ward off evil spirits.

Once again, the debate emerges: "What amount of culture did Africans bring with them to the New World?" Numerous island rituals, customs, and folktales leave little doubt concerning African retentions. However, while agreeing that the motor behavior in rituals such as the ring dance retain strong elements from West African culture, the question of meaning still remains. Although the spirituals can be understood only when viewed in the context of the African-styled dances, the island ring dance ritual can only be fully comprehended if one takes seriously the Christian motifs found in the spirituals.[12] Naturally, islanders continued to use recognized African dance movements, but after 1800, as Sea Islanders converted to Christianity, new meanings were infused into their ancient ritual forms.

Using an "evolutionary" analogy, one could ask, "How do you define a new species?" It is simple. If you take samples of fish and isolate them for enough generations, and then put them back with the old fish, they may look similar but they can no longer reproduce with the old fish. You have a new species.[13] Culturally speaking, in the early 1800s, slaves in the United States ceased to be Africans and became African Americans. Similar rites existed between the two but the meanings had all changed.

When examining the new meaning of these old rituals, a key question is whether Gullahs continued to understand the ring dance and shout to be religious in nature. In 1862, older islanders told William Gannett that "they did not like the shouts, or think them religious." In fact, they distrusted the entire ceremony. Laura Towne reported visiting the pray's house for worship but afterwards attending "the shout, a savage heathenish dance out in Rina's house." Charlotte Forten questioned the islanders concerning the shout's religious nature and some residents told her it possessed none. Despite these protests, most islanders practiced shouting, and most frequently they performed the ritual at pray's houses after the prayer meeting:

> After the praise meeting is over, there usually follows the very singular and impressive performance of the shout, or religious dance of the negroes. Three or four, standing still, clapping their hands and beating time with their feet, commence singing . . . while the others walk around in a ring.[14]

How can one explain these contradictions? It appears there existed two shouts. The first represents a clear African survival practiced in the slave quarters. In many ways, it was a social dance evolving out of African ritual. During the 1830s and 1840s, Methodist and Baptist missionaries labored to eradicate these dances. Charles Lyell recounted in 1849 that "on the Hopeton plantation above twenty violins have been silenced by the Methodist missionaries."

Despite this opposition to social dances, evangelicals allowed and even encouraged another dance style.

> At the Methodist prayer-meetings, they are permitted to move rapidly in a ring, joining hands in token of brotherly love, presenting first the right hand and then the left . . . as a substitute for the dance.

After an islander converted to Christianity and entered the pray's house community, she no longer practiced the worldly dances in the cabins where "de sinners cross um feet." Instead, she danced to the spiritual tunes. Indicating two types of shouting, Old Binah, a spiritual leader on Saint Helena in 1862, stated that she did not object to the dances at the pray's house but "did not like the shout out in de world." Pulitzer Prize-winner Julia Peterkin wrote about an island woman recently converted:

> She missed dancing, and whenever she heard the big drum beating and the accordion wailing she felt sad, but shouting at prayer-meeting was pleasure and old hymns and spirituals were

> beautiful. When the people all sang . . . she joined in and felt so
> holy that cold chills ran up and down her spine.

There were two types of dancing. The old social dances continued but the island churches expected members to avoid these. Only the church sanctioned dance rituals, initiated by missionaries in the 1830s, were approved. No longer African in meaning, the meassage of the new dance was discovered in the spirituals which taught a theology built around the cross and resurrection of Jesus. In their daily lives Black islanders well understood Jesus' suffering, and at night, at the pray's house, they could experience his resurrection. In ecstatic shouts and in trance states, islanders left behind their old lives and entered into Christ's glory.

> The old meeting house caught on fire. The spirit was there. Every heart was beating in unison as we turned our minds to God to tell him of our sorrows here below. God saw our need and came to us. . . . there is a joy on the inside and it wells up so strong that we can't keep still. It is fire in the bones. Any time that fire touches a man, he will jump.[15]

Having emphasized Saint Helena's conversion from an African religious base to a Christian one, it is important to state that these two world views need not always stand in opposition to one another. Many similarities exist between traditional African beliefs and Christianity. Both possess moral values and rituals that emphasize community and communicate faith to practitioners. Both consider God to be good, merciful and all powerful.[16] In addition, while most-often labeled a European faith by modern secular critics, early Christianity actual evolved in a Middle Eastern and North African context. Important Church fathers such as Antony, Tertullian, Origen, and Augustine made their homes in Africa. Scholarship that only poses oppositional questions between African religions and Christianity will never fully appreciate Sea Island culture.

Within these ecstactic African rites converted to Christianity, islanders personally found a conversion experience. In stark contrast with the Yankee missionaries who emphasized gradual Christian nurture, Saint Helena islanders understood conversion as an immediate crisis event. Each year individual islanders, most often young people, heard God's call and entered into an initiation period. Through the dramatic, elaborate rituals that surrounded conversion, an islander became a member of the community. It is difficult to overemphasize conversion's importance among the islanders. This crisis, known in some churches as "catching sense," defined a person's very existence in the community.[17]

In continuity with their African heritage, Saint Helena islanders emphasized a crisis conversion, which served many functions strikingly similar to West African community initiation rituals. Through induction rituals, one passed from childhood to adulthood. In seclusion, spiritual elders instructed the candidate about faith, tradition, and cultural matters which equipped him or her to live as a full member in the society. Initiation demonstrated unity with the community and served as a bridge into the supernatural world, enabling one to participate in the community's sacred rituals.[18]

Methodist workers first introduced Christian "seeking" rituals in the 1830s when they instructed the slaves to "seek Jesus" and placed candidates on trial until they seemed fully prepared for baptism. This preparation time involved religious instruction and an examination of the candidate's life in response to certain questions. Eventually, Methodist "seeking" rituals combined with earlier African visionary quests to become Saint Helena's traditional conversion method.

Seeking commenced after an initial spiritual experience which might occur during a sermon, in the midst of a conversation, or even in a field. One seeker reported:

> The first time I heard the voice I was in the cotton patch. A voice said, "Behold, I move you by the still waters." The voice was like muttering thunder. I kept on praying. . . .[19]

Despite current writers who downplay the role of sin and repentance in Sea Island conversion experiences, the records demonstrate that these standard Christian doctrines held a strong place in the island "seeking" ritual. One man told his story:

> De odder night I was sittin' by de fire, an' I 'gin thinkin'. After a while I 'gin a feelin' bad. I's done bin to prayer meetin', an' I sort a 'gin feelin' bad dere. . . . Seem like dere was a big load a pressin' me down . . . when de mornin' comes I got no better. . . . Wat mus I do? . . . Dese sins kill me. Dey press me till I dead. . . . All de folks say, Wat's de matter? An' I couldn't tell, I feel so pressed. Den

Uncle Pete, he come see me; tell me I mus pray. Den I goes out into de field; I pray dere.

Island spirituals also emphasized the connection between the seeking ritual in the wilderness and the forgiveness of sins:

Jesus set poor sinners free.
Way down in the valley.
Who will rise and go with me?
Cry holy, holy.
Look at de people dat is born of God.
And I ran down de valley, and I run down to pray.
Say, look at de people dat is born of God.

Following a person's initial call by God, seeking involved a vision quest supervised by a spiritual guide. More often than not, spiritual guides were women holding significant authority in Saint Helena's culture. In 1862 missionary Harriet Ware stated that "old Peggy and Binah were the two whom all that came into the church had to come through, and the church supports them." Laura Towne mentioned Maum Katie, over 100 years old, a great "spiritual mother" with "tremendous influence over her spiritual children."[20]

The spiritual guide provided catechism for the seeker and, most important, sent him "into the wilderness" for the vision quest. Time and again, the seeker returned to relate his vision only to be sent back into the woods or swamp. The guide claimed secret knowledge from God, a "password" which the seeker must attain in order to demonstrate conversion. Until the seeker reported a vision that fit the guide's password, he would not be received. Military commander T. W. Higginson wrote about islanders on a vision quest:

"De Valley and de lonesome valley" were familiar words in their religious experience. To descend into that region implied the same process with the "anxious seat" of the camp meeting. When a young girl was supposed to enter it, she bound a handkerchief by a particular knot over her head, and made it a point of honor not to change a single garment till the day of her baptism, so that she was sure of being in physical readiness for the cleansing rite. . . . More than once, in noticing a damsel thus mystically kerchiefed, I asked some dusky attendant its meaning, and received the unfailing answer. . . . He in de lonesome valley, sa.[21]

Islanders understood that "in the wilderness" or "in the valley" God most clearly communicated with them. Even years after their vision quest, church elders prayed for guidance from God and asked Jesus to teach them "as he [did] in de woods." In the wilderness, a seeker spent long hours in prayer attempting to "get through," and almost all other activities ceased during the initiation ritual. Missionary Elizabeth Botume complained about the disturbance in the school routine:

In the winter most of the children were seeking and praying. . . . they were not allowed to do much of anything else for fear they would be turned back.

One woman said of her adopted daughter, "She has been hanging her head and trying to pray these three months, and she hasn't got through yet, and she don't want to do nothing in all this time. . . .

The young seekers were in a stupid and lethargic condition. They began by wearing the most ragged and untidy clothing, and they often tied dirty bands around their heads, literally putting on sackcloth and ashes. Some children were not allowed to come to school for fear they would be turned back.

A Methodist missionary writing before the war gave a lengthy report:

When one of these people becomes serious, or "begins to pray" as he would say—and this is seldom the result of preaching, but most commonly "a warning in a dream,"—it is customary for him to select . . . some church member of influence, as his spiritual guide. Females are often chosen. Soon after the vision in which his teacher is pointed out, he . . . puts himself under his instruction. These are of a two-fold nature . . . He is now a prophet to teach him how to conduct himself, and particularly how to pray. He is also "an interpreter of visions" to whom the seeker relates all his "travel." This word travel . . . comprehends all those exercises, spiritual, visionary, and imaginative, which make up an experience. . . . When the teacher is satisfied with the travel of the seeker, he pronounces "he git thru"; and he is ready for the church. This decision is never questioned by the neophyte. "I prayed under him," says the latter; "he is my spiritual father."[22]

Seeking was serious work for the islanders and success was never assured. Ellen Murray and Laura Towne met a woman over one hundred years old who had "tried to pray all her life, but was always turned back." Finally, on January 28, 1877, "she was triumphantly baptized, with all her family about her."[23]

As with this elderly woman, when a seeker ultimately "got through," she prepared for the dramatic baptism ritual. Laura Towne wrote:

After church, Father Tom and his bench of elders examined the candidates for baptism and asked Ellen [Murray] to record their names. . . . Each candidate, clothed in the oldest possible clothes and with a handkerchief made into a band and tied around the forehead, stood humbly before the bench. Father Tom looking like Jupiter himself . . . put the most posing questions, to which the candidates replied meekly and promptly. He asked the satisfactory candidate at last, "How do you pray?" Then the soft, musical voices made the coaxing, entreating kind of prayer they use so much. A nod dismissed the applicant and another was called up. There were sixty or seventy to examine.

"You think you are converted?"

"Yes, . . . I so lovin! I loves ebery body—all de trees, an' de chicken, an de' peoples; I loves ebery ting an' ebery body."

"Why do you wish to join the church?"

"De Bible tell us to join de church."

"Why do you wish to be baptized?"

"De Lord Jesus was baptized."[24]

Baptisms occurred each quarter during a long Sunday's celebration with islanders bringing their lunch to the gala event. Missionary David Thorpe, in an 1863 letter, emphasized that "They all insist upon immersion . . . Sprinkling wouldn't do, none at all." Even Methodists on the islands sought baptism by immersion. Other than the baptism candidates, who dressed in rags, everyone wore their finest clothes, bright scarves and turbans decorating the women's heads. The ritual occurred outdoors at a local creek and when the last person burst from the water, the attending crowd broke into song as they marched back to the church. Thorpe wrote:

> The candidates came ready dressed for the waters. Every one had their head tied up in a Handkerchief . . . nearly all of them were dressed in miserable clothing. . . . After Mr. Phillips, the Minister has read their names and they had responded, and Old Pa Tom had nodded his approval to their examination, the Pastor . . . [led them] to the creek. Together they entered the water. . . . They immersed them, over one hundred and forty. As fast as they had been baptized they stepped to the shore . . . their friends received them . . . and hurried them off into the bushes. . . . All the candidates came out in shiny robes . . . there was a great difference in their looks when they came into the church the second time. Then we had a long service after which . . . the sacrament [communion] was administered to them.[25]

Following the baptism service, the community looked on the young person as a full member of society, and the convert's white baptismal robe "was put away in the bottom of the cupboard to be used for her shroud when she died."[26]

What remained when the conversion rites ended? The goal of Gullah Christianity was to support the believer in the midst of a difficult life, ensuring that true Christians exhibited faith regardless of the circumstances. To complain or express doubt showed lack of faith, the unforgivable sin. Elizabeth Botume wrote:

> Early in the week I went to see Katy . . . to console her for the loss of her only child. Instead of finding her sad, she was almost jubilant . . . she said, "You know, ma'am, the Big Massa want him. Him been a-callin' him fur long time."
> . . . Another little girl in the school died. . . . I said to her father, "I am so sorry you have lost Rossa."
> "Oh, we mustn't say that," he answered with a broad smile. "We mustn't fly in the face of Providence. The Massa call my lee-

tle gal, an' him mus' go. Ef him call him, him want him, an' us can't say nothing."

In one cabin I found a man in a most wretched condition. Years before he had fallen from a building and broken his back. . . . He was left alone and destitute, a most repulsive object. . . . I had his cabin cleaned and whitewashed, and fresh, clean clothes put on the poor fellow. . . . In all my interviews with him I never heard a word of complaint, although his sufferings must have been extreme.

"Bless the Lord, missis!" he said, "tain't no use to fret about it, for it can't be helpt. . . . Sometimes at night I'se so painful I can't shet my eye, an' den I look out de doah, up at the stars, an' t'ink dem de eyes of de Lord looking straight down at me one. An' I 'member . . . De Lord is my Shepherd, I shall not want; for in course I is His little sheep, an' I is so glad! It 'pears like the pain don't hurt me no more."[27]

Some Yankee missionaries expressed concern over the seemingly apathetic and fatalistic attitudes found on the island. In reality, Gullahs found in Christianity a reason for being in the midst of oppression and suffering. Through their deep identification with Jesus Christ and his cross, they developed a collective strength, a cultural tenacity and the ability to withstand suffering. Despite their own pain, Christ had suffered more, and just as his cross brought salvation, their sufferings would carry them to glory.

Islanders placed a premium on trusting in God in the midst of suffering. While the missionaries' liberal Protestantism understood faith in terms of victorious progress and activism, Gullah evangelicalism interpreted faith as trust and survival. On his nights of deep pain, Botume's crippled man found solace in his prayers, and when he returned from his mystic meditations of staring into the eyes of God among the stars, somehow his pain had vanished. Even when death knocked at the door, the sick confessed, "I have made up my mind to leave all with God. He will not put more on me than I can bear."

Nineteenth-century African Americans were surrounded by uncertainties, broken promises, and contradictions, but the Christian God became a fixed point of reference in their shifting world. All Christ demanded was faith without any doubts. When asked how suffering could exist if God was good, one old black man angrily shouted, "Son, I put that doubt behind me long ago."[28]

Regardless of their sufferings, Christ remained the same, and he stood beside them, suffered and wept with them. The doctrine of "Emmanuel, God with us," as found in Matthew's gospel and the prophet Isaiah, attained great importance among the Gullah. Surrounded often by hellish conditions, Gullahs remained strong because they believed Christ stood beside them. Marcus, an island preacher, told Laura Towne:

> They [islanders] never knew what would befall them, and poor black folks could only wait and have faith. . . . his massa had laughed and asked him once whether he thought Christ was going to take damned black niggers into heaven. He felt sure of one thing, that they would be where Christ was, and even if that was in hell, it would be a heaven, for it did not matter what place they were in if they were only with Christ.[29]

Following the Civil War, church membership soared on the Sea Islands. Prior to the war, many slave owners denied church membership to their slaves, thus enhancing membership's value in the Gullahs' eyes. During the 1860s, Saint Helena residents flocked to the baptismal waters seeking entrance into the faith community. This community emphasis was vitally important; one could not be a Christian alone.

Pulling any and all lost sheep inside the fold, communal life offered forgiveness regardless of the sin. Mainland legal authorities sentenced one island man to the penitentiary, but when his term ended, the religious community gave a party in his honor, and welcomed him back into the fold like the prodigal son. In the same fashion, this life together in the church required the same communal forgiveness from members. Two women, Rina and Celia, were angry with one another. Since Celia stood outside the community, Rina could hold her grudge. When Celia re-entered the church, the community expected reconciliation between the two women.[30]

The church's common life meant more than mere words of reconciliation. Following the war, religious collective aid societies formed among African Americans throughout Beaufort County's islands to assist poor neighbors. Missionary T. D. Howard wrote on this "mutuality of helpfulness" found on the island.

> In Beaufort . . . there are eleven organizations . . . bearing such names as "Sons and Daughters of Zion," "Rising Sons and Daughters of Zion," and "The Mary and Martha Society." The last mentioned association has . . . five hundred dollars in the treasury. The ordinary allowance during sickness is fifty cents a week.
>
> . . . What has been the efficient cause of and support in this wonderful change? . . . the institutions of religion . . . Amid all things transient, and in the great change emancipation has wrought, the Church with its fellowship and ordinances has been the one thing permanent . . . those united in church fellowship are usually banded for mutual assistance. The congregation is a community; if one member suffers, the other members relieve.[31]

Gullahs could not understand the individualism of the missionaries' New England religion because if one did not belong to a family and a community then one had no place in the world. An island woman questioning Yankee Arthur Sumner left the room confused:

> "How many children you got, Misser Sumner," . . .
> "Not one, thank the Lord."
> "No Chillun?"
> "I'm not married."
> In sheer amazement she sat down and stared at me. . . . "Oh, you'r joking. . . . Not married! Why . . . you looked settled. . . . You a member sure?"
> "Eh?"
> "A member, a church member."
> "Neither married nor a member," I replied with solemn voice.
> She almost dropped my breakfast.[32]

Amazingly, this communal life of love and forgiveness extended even to the former plantation owners. Gabriel Capus, a slave holder, returned in 1865 with no money and nothing to eat. Rina received him into her home and he lived there a few weeks. Rina was "greatly exercised upon this question of the return of the old masters." She felt no desire to work for the man again, but neither could she leave him abandoned in the street. Her ethical

code and compassion prevented such callous behavior. On another plantation, black islanders collected one hundred dollars for their former owner
now in poverty. Northern reporters at Port Royal expressed amazement and
discovered that although the former slaves feared the slaveholders, they also
felt "genuine commiseration for them in their distress."[33] Once again, Christ
had suffered even more for them and yet He forgave them their sins. How
could they do less for the former slave holders?

Throughout the twentieth century, scholars have commented on religion's centrality on the Sea Islands. All agree that the church and pray's
houses were the dominant institutions, but despite these affirmations, few
have explored the reasons behind this dominance over the culture. The
church's premium value placed on forgiveness, hospitality, and charity, and
its life interpretation regarding Christ's presence in suffering held the people
together in a tight community during extremely difficult times. While the rituals of the missionaries' religion demonstrated commitment to individual
achievement and progress, the Gullah islanders chose to reinforce those
Christian doctrines that emphasized community and tradition. Their most
holy rituals were reserved for members. Only the faithful participated in the
shout and ring dances. Others watched from outside the circle. Furthermore,
Gullahs tended to be "closed communion Baptists" and this fact sparked significant controversy in the 1860s.[34]

While the islanders greatly appreciated the missionaries' arrival in 1862,
conflict arose that summer concerning their participation in the communion
service. After "much talk and trouble about this," the church elders decided
to bar "all who were not Baptists" from the Lord's table. Some elders became
so "excited" about the missionaries receiving communion that they would
not allow the teachers to remain in the building while the supper was served.
Having traveled so far to aid the freedmen, the missionaries now felt
shunned. The issue was debated until 1864 when a new Baptist minister,
Reverend Parker, expressed "liberal views towards other denominations of
Christians, and then invited all members of sister churches to remain to the
communion service." The conflict immediately exploded. Reverend Parker
left the church and Elder Demas informed Ellen Murray that he wished "all
the white people would go to the white church and worship together and
leave the black alone in their own brick church." A few church members
attempted to alter the policy but met resistance from church elders. Towne
wrote:

> Nelly had today . . . a long talk with Demas upon close com-
> munion, but he was immovable, as might be supposed. He did
> not think much of the theological arguments of a girl like Nelly.

Demas Washington became the pastor of Brick Baptist in late 1864 and since most members at the church preferred closed communion, the missionaries reconciled themselves to that fact. Laura Towne felt hurt for many years. Even in 1877, she expressed tremendous gratitude toward a black Methodist minister who included her in the communion service.[35]

What created this impassable divide? Theological concerns drove the debate. Baptists across the South were notoriously closed communion advocates, believing the ordinance was strictly for baptized church members. Gullah Baptists understood and followed the same doctrines. Significantly, island Methodists tended to practice open communion. That had been the Methodist doctrine since the time of John Wesley, who understood the sacrament as a means of grace to God for everyone who would receive it. However, beyond the theological debate was the religious community's need to maintain its internal integrity. Most Gullahs considered community membership vitally important because years of suffering together in slavery had formed that community. Exclusiveness served collective goals and expressed loyalty, solidarity, and trust. The uninitiated remained outsiders even if they were the beloved missionary school teachers.[36]

Ethical behavior among the Gullah also tended to be communal, not individual, in orientation. The missionaries wrote extensively concerning the islanders' ethical deficiencies. For Northern Protestants, individual ethics stood at the heart of Christianity and they stated that the Gullah's "morals, like his religion, belong to an arrested stage, a backward era." While the black church overlooked stealing a chicken, attending a "worldly" dance might bring punishment. A man with three wives might remain a member in good standing but one who refused to forgive his neighbor would be dismissed. The missionaries raged against the islanders' "skill in lying, their great reticence, their habit of shielding one another," but these were merely the skills of survival in a slave's world. Some evidence suggests that only offenses within the community were considered sins. Prior to the war, stealing from outsiders, especially the white slave holders, was not a sin. A Methodist minister, Thomas Turpin, observed a pre-war slave religious service where communicants were instructed "never to divulge the secret of stealing" lest they face censure from the faith community.[37] Unlike the abstract ethics of progress found in the missionary religion, the Gullah faith community's ethics revolved around loyalty to the fellowship and caring for one another.

Most of the mission workers abandoned the island in frustration labeling the Gullahs as hopelessly unethical—"at least, in the present generation"—but a few, like William Gannett, expressed deep appreciation for the communal life of the island:

> We live on our friends in a great many ways here. Without attempting any system or intending to set a wrong world right, we realize all the best fruits of socialistic communities. If anyone has anything good, he is expected to enjoy only a small piece himself; and most things that are done have a reference to our united, not to any individual interest. [November 1864][38]

While Gullahs maintained many of their earlier religious values, the dramatic events surrounding emancipation forever changed Saint Helena's history and culture. In the wake of the war, there emerged the new values of freedom, land ownership, and education. Among the islanders, the war and their new life took on a religious quality. Following Lincoln's death, Laura Towne wrote about the absolute religious nature of these events in the minds of the islanders:

> Saturday, April 29, 1865. It was a frightful blow at first. The people have refused to believe he was dead. . . . One man asked me in a whisper if it were true that the "Government was dead." Rina says she can't sleep for thinking how sorry she is to lose "Pa Linkum." You know they call their elders in the church—or the particular one who converted and received them in—their spiritual father. . . . these fathers are addressed with fear and awe as "Pa Marcus," "Pa Demas."[39]

Like their freedom, forbidden to the islanders for so long, literacy carried an almost mystical power and was shrouded in superstition. "Negroes . . . almost worshiped the Bible, and their anxiety to read it was their greatest incentive to learn." The Gullahs longed to read the Bible for themselves rather than depending on a white man's interpretation, and islanders, adults and children, arrived daily at the school with Bible in hand "asking to be taught to read."[40]

Penn School used the scriptures everyday in the curriculum, imparting a religious atmosphere to the educational proceedings. After only a few months in the classroom, the children instinctively knew that literacy imparted spiritual power. While attending a funeral, Harriet Ware watched in fascination as the children enacted a new religious ritual:

> As we drew near the grave we heard all the children singing their A, B, C, through and through again, as they stood waiting round the grave for the rest to assemble. . . . Each child had his school-book . . . in his hand . . . they consider their lessons as in some sort a religious exercise.[41]

This new spirituality of education taught at the Penn School carried sufficient power to alter other, older religious rituals on the island. During the antebellum period and in the early 1860s, "seeking" occurred in the winter. Such a schedule conformed to the plantation work environment where winter offered young people enough free time to spend in the wilderness. Under a school schedule, winter did not offer the best time-frame. Throughout the 1860s, children endured the conflicting demands of the seeking traditions and those of the school. Finally, spiritual guides resolved the problem, and the summer months, when school was not in session, became the proper time for seeking. Once again, the islanders demonstrated the ability to maintain the old while embracing the new.[42]

With each passing year, the islanders, aided by the missionaries, made great educational strides. Prior to the war, the slaves of the Sea Islands were considered the most isolated and uneducated of all slaves. However, in the late 1880s, an election demonstrated amazing changes. In a near-by voting precinct, only seven out of 113 men could sign their name. All others merely made their mark. In the precinct served by the Penn School, 69 out of 72 men signed their names.[43]

In others ways, the Penn School religion failed to attract converts. Islanders never understood the Yankee religion and preferred the stirring emotional sermons provided by local black preachers. One island woman said:

> I goes ter some churches, an' I sees folks settin' quiet an' still, like dey dunno what the Holy Sperit am . . . dey tells us we mustn't make no noise ter praise de Lord. I don't want no sich 'ligion as dat ar.[44]

By the mid-1870s, Saint Helena's ex-slaves had acquired most of the land on the island and settled into a new pattern of life. Other than the school teachers and a few shop keepers, African Americans composed the entire population on the island. Coastal Carolina's economy improved during the 1880s and the islanders began building themselves a comfortable existence. Cotton remained the primary cash crop on Saint Helena while rice continued to flourish on neighboring islands. In addition, phosphate mining provided new jobs. Their isolation spared the islanders the harsh backlash that followed the Reconstruction years. While other African Americans suffered under a renewed domination, the Gullahs lived alone and unmolested. Their lives were certainly modest, but by the early 1890s, the agriculture and mining industry had brought a prosperity never previously known to the Gullahs.

Then the world ended. On August 28, 1893, the fiercest hurricane to hit the southern coast in modern history passed directly over the island. Earlier that week, several storms grazed the coastline, but on Friday, August 25 warnings traveled up the eastern seaboard that a tremendous storm stood off the Florida coast and was surging northwest. The Sea Islanders, who possessed no telegraph, never received the warning. By Sunday afternoon, everyone recognized the danger signs, since they had seen many hurricanes. They had never seen one like this. Near midnight, the wind reached 120 m.p.h. and the tide rose 19 feet above sea level, completely washing over the low-lying islands. Margaret Weary, an island resident, related the following story:

> I was so busy that evening cooking supper I never minded the wind and rain, nor the great roaring of the waves, till I looked out through the shutter and saw the sea all around the house. . . . Ma seized my little sister Grace, wrapped her in a blanket and ran to a neighbor's house on the hill. Brother and I jumped into the water and ran as fast as we could, but I fell down. . . . My brother picked me up, and we pressed on through the waves till we reached the house. . . . The water had come up all around that house too, so we had to run to another, up on higher land, and there stayed all night.

At the storm's height, a great tidal wave washed across the island moving inland with tremendous force and then in its return motion, sucked everything in its path out to sea. In all, an estimated three to five thousand people drowned on the Sea Islands and the tempest left 30,000 homeless. Margaret Weary wrote:

> Next morning we went home, but there was no house there, nor anything left. All had been washed away. . . . We saw dead cats and dogs, dead horses and hogs all along the shore, and some dead men and women and children.[45]

The next few months proved atrocious. With the salt water driven twenty miles up the low country's rivers, crops were ruined, leaving the people little to no food for the year. Refugees crowded into Penn School seeking shelter. Red Cross leader Clara Barton had served on the Carolina coast during the Civil War as a missionary and she eagerly returned there, establishing a Red Cross headquarters in Beaufort.

Northerners who had long forgotten the Port Royal experiment suddenly remembered the Sea Islanders. Medicines, food, clothing, and tools arrived. Former missionary Edward Pierce paid to rebuild a small library on Saint Helena and sent a thousand books to replace those destroyed in the storm's aftermath. Men went to work rebuilding homes while women organized into sewing teams to make clothing. Freshly dug ditches crisscrossed the islands and drained the sea water from the fields.

Despite the assistance and hardwork, many aspects of nineteenth-century life vanished, washed forever out to sea. The storm destroyed the phosphate mining operations and the industry never returned. The hurricane consumed the massive irrigation complex supporting the rice industry. Built over hundreds of years on the back of slave labor, this canal system, which had been compared in complexity to the pyramids of Egypt, was never rebuilt and the rice plantations ended.

With their past washed away, the islanders stood on the edge of the twentieth century. Two factors remained constant: one was a commitment to community, to aiding their brothers and sisters. The second constant was a persistent faith that the suffering Christ lived with them in their hardships on this lonely island. Regardless of their pain, Jesus had endured more and now he lived among them, more real than their closest neighbors. A teacher wrote:

> Calling one day at a rickety cabin, with dirt floor, no chimney, and large holes in the roof . . . the old woman who lived there—

all her relations were dead—hobbled to the door. "You live here all alone, Aunt Phillis?" She answered instantly, and simply as a child, "Me and Jesus, Massa. Me and Jesus."[46]

4

The Mission Expands

31 OCTOBER 1904: Despite the island's hot humid air, Frances Butler reclined on her bed shivering as her fever mounted ever higher. Constantly by her side, Rossa Cooley washed Butler's face with cool wet cloths. The two teachers had resided at the Penn School for less than a month, making bold plans for a center of Christian progressive education, but neither fully recognized the extent of their isolation until malaria struck Frances Butler. As the situation grew worse, Cooley sent for the army doctor at Fort Fremont, located on the island's opposite side. Upon arrival, the physician dispatched orders to Beaufort for medical supplies but this required another six mile ride and a boat crossing on the wide Beaufort River. Late that night, Butler looked up at Cooley and said, "I'm so glad we came here." Far from her family and friends in the north, Frances Butler died at the Penn School on November 1, 1904. The *Boston Evening Transcript* eulogized Butler as a pioneer in American missionary work, resounding with a "thrill of pride" concerning the enthusiasm of "those who give their lives in the missionary field."[1]

Soon another woman, Grace Bigelow House joined Rossa Cooley. House told Cooley that she would stay at Penn for a year and then join her parents who served as missionaries in Turkey. That one year commitment lasted forty. During that time, Cooley and House dramatically improved the island's educational and health system while also working for economic renewal and racial equality. As the years passed, however, their vision expanded to include ever larger fields of endeavor. Seeking the Kingdom of God on Earth, they imagined that they could change the world from their lonely island outpost.

From 1900 to 1950, Penn School became a small part in a worldwide mission effort seeking to "save the world in our generation." Linked with such movements as the YMCA and the social gospel, and inspired by progressive and industrial education ideals, Penn preached the "abundant life" and a message of servanthood to all humanity. Long before John F. Kennedy asked a similar question, Rossa Cooley challenged her students saying, "Too often we ask what our church, our school, our faith can do for us, instead of what we can do for them. Jesus meets us . . . by asking, what will you do for me and them?"[2] Visitors from major universities and dignitaries from foreign nations praised Penn as a model educational facility.

Penn's twentieth century road to success had been well paved in the late nineteenth century by Laura Towne, Ellen Murray, and countless African-American church leaders on the island. Since the early 1860s, the Penn School had developed an educated citizenry on Saint Helena, setting it apart from most of the rural South. Furthermore, the island's continued isolation had shielded residents from much oppression and helped maintain a strong spiritual culture governed by the church's "just law." The promise of better days seemed certain.

> "Chile, chile, why ain't you ben gib me dat promise?" muttered the sick man [beaten badly by his owner] . . . to the little girl who raised a trembling little black hand. "I, Better Days . . . do hereby solemnly promise to consecrate my life to de revengement of my father, Prophet Hosea, an' to de upliftment of my race. . . ."
>
> "Amen and Amen," repeated the dying man. . . .
>
> Fifty years had changed the eager-faced little girl to an eager-faced woman. . . . Better Days did not forget her promise and for many years had been teaching in one of the country schools. . . .
>
> "What did you do about your promise to revenge your father's death?" asked the lady. "I done study dat matter for a long time till one Sunday I hear de preacher read from de Book, 'Vengeance is mine, I will repay, saith de Lord.' . . . It look to me like de Lord done his business mos' effectual. All de family of ole massa done perish off de face of de earth in sorrow . . . So," ended Better Days with her happy laugh, "here I is, still a-workin' out my promise for de uplift of my people. . . . I jes holds to my poor little light an' does my work de best I know how. An'

some time de Lord will send a big shining light that will 'spell de shadows from all de corners of dis land an' all de world will live in de light of de knowledge of God. Sometimes when . . . I thinks of our grand school . . . it seem like de big light am beginning to shine already on St. Helena."[3]

Better days certainly seemed on the horizon, but, in 1900, Towne and Murray were in their seventies and suffering from health problems. Therefore, Towne invited Dr. Hollis Frissell, the visionary leader of Hampton Institute in Virginia, to visit Saint Helena and provide guidance for Penn's future. Viewed by many Americans as the premier expert in African-American pedagogy, Frissell held a boundless faith in humanity's potential moral progress. With a "vivid consciousness of the Divine Purpose that rules the universe," Frissell optimistically believed that peace and goodwill among men would "ultimately conquer all prejudice and hatred."[4]

On December 31, 1900, a small assembly gathered on Saint Helena to assume leadership at the school. As Towne lay dying in her bed, she passed the mantle of responsibility to a board of trustees. Besides her life-long colleague Ellen Murray, the new board consisted of Dr. Hollis Frissell, Towne's niece, Mrs. William Jenks, as well as her son Robert Jenks, fresh from Harvard Law School, and J. R. McDonald, a transplanted Yankee operating a general store on the island. Soon to join the board were idealistic philanthropists George Foster Peabody, Francis Cope, Jr., and Arthur Curtiss James.[5]

Frissell regarded Saint Helena and the Penn School as a perfect laboratory for an experiment in educational salvation. On this isolated island among residents of full African descent, Hollis Frissell found a control group to prove to the nation that African Americans could become full productive citizens. Penn would serve not simply as a school for educating Saint Helena's children, but as an "opportunity to work out a plan for industrial education that would help the entire rural South."[6]

Despite the rapid moves made by the new board following Towne's death in 1901, Rossa Cooley did not arrive on the island until 1904. Initially, Frissell recommended "a good colored man to go down there, look into the work, and if possible introduce some new methods."[7] The trustees hired P. W. Dawkins, a black teacher from Kittrell College, to serve as Penn's new director while Ellen Murray continued as principal only in name. Upon arrival, Dawkins inaugurated among the island's landowners many agricultural programs that became standard features at Penn during the next four decades.

African-American landownership was among Saint Helena's primary saving graces, and it set it apart from most of the South. On nearby Johns Island, white planters owned the land and African Americans sharecropped for these planters each year. Even in the early twentieth century, these contracts bound the entire family—husband, wife, and children—to labor in the fields as virtual slaves. For their labor they received living quarters and staple foods that could not be grown in their garden plots. During the working months, children attended school only on rainy days "but if by noon the sun came out, the plantation overseer would ride up to school and call for the tenants' children."[8] In contrast to such abject poverty, Saint Helena residents owned their small farms and enjoyed life as poor but secure yeomen.

In this setting, Dawkins began his visionary work for a community of cooperative farmers. Following Booker T. Washington's lead at Tuskegee Institute, he organized a Farmers' Conference for moral, educational, and economic improvement. Dawkins's message was simple and clear:

> Don't fail to have money in your pockets when you go home; don't let merchants and agents talk you into buying what you don't need . . . don't make debts you don't mean to pay. . . . Don't expect to drink milk and honey over yonder and not try to make an honest living here . . . don't keep your children out of school.[9]

For three years, Dawkins provided leadership for the new Penn School, and there exists no evidence that he failed in any way. In fact, two years after he arrived, the trustees recommended the "necessity and advisability of increasing the scope of Mr. Dawkins' work and authority." They increased his salary, and Francis Cope "urged that . . . the Superintendent of Industries [Dawkins] be given wider power." The board approved Cope's proposal.[10] Everything seemed positive. Nevertheless, Dawkins's position as Penn's primary leader came to an abrupt end.

In 1903, Penn's trustees sought financial assistance from the General Education Board, founded the previous year by John D. Rockefeller for the promotion of education. When Wallace Buttrick of the GEB visited Saint Helena to assess the Penn School, he felt disturbed by Ellen Murray's resistance to the changing program. Seeking to speed up Penn's advancement under Dawkins, Buttrick recommended Ellen Murray's removal as quickly

but as painlessly as possible. These developments concerning Penn's matri-
archal, original founder created a controversial storm. Robert Jenks and
Francis Cope believed that Dawkins could manage these problems with
Murray; however, Frissell had altered his opinion. He no longer felt that
Dawkins or any black man could manage the transfer. With deep concern,
Jenks wrote to Cope saying:

> When I arrived at Hampton Dr. Frissell told me at once that he
> could not approve our plan for building up the industrial
> department under Mr. Dawkins . . . he did not believe any negro
> could make a success out of the plan which we proposed. I felt
> that we ought to accept Dr. Frissell's opinion as that of an expert.
> . . . I think that Dawkins can do very valuable work . . . but Dr.
> Frissell says . . . that it seems wiser to keep him under white con-
> trol. Dr. Frissell said confidentially that even at Tuskegee under
> Mr. Washington himself the defects of negro control are very
> apparent. This remark you will not repeat to anyone.[11]

During this meeting, Frissell recommended "Miss R. B. Cooley, a woman
of about 30 years of age and a graduate of Vassar College, and Miss Butler,
her assistant." Rossa B. Cooley, a Presbyterian, had spent her youth in
Poughkeepsie, New York, where her father taught physics at Vassar College.
After graduating from Vassar, Cooley taught school for eight years, six of
them at Hampton. In winter 1902, Cooley and Butler toured the southern
United States, including three days on Saint Helena, studying the educational problems in the area. After an interview with Cooley, Jenks expressed
his belief that she could "renovate" Miss Murray and "gradually, but firmly,
change her standards." Cooley on her part pledged to undertake the work
"in the true missionary spirit."[12]

Thus, Rossa Cooley and Frances Butler found themselves on Saint
Helena Island as leaders of the Penn School. For Butler, it proved to be a
short-lived mission and her body returned home within a month. For
Cooley, the journey began a life-long commitment to the educational salvation of the islanders.

Following Frances Butler's death, Grace Bigelow House joined Cooley
on Saint Helena. Miss House was born on the Mediterranean mission field
where her parents served as missionaries in Greece and Turkey. A graduate
of Columbia University Teachers College, Grace House firmly believed in

the progressive education creed made famous by such luminaries as John Dewey and William Kilpatrick. A poet and an idealist, House possessed a deeply reflective spirituality revealed throughout her extensive diaries. Each year on New Year's Eve, she wrote her prayer:

> Forgetting those things which are behind, and reaching forth unto those things which are before, I press toward the mark for the prize of the high calling of God in Jesus Christ. This is my text for the new year. God help me press forward without flinching for Jesus Christ's sake.[13]

Grace House eagerly wanted to make her mark on the world. Her diary entries repeatedly demonstrate a concern that time was passing quickly and that she had accomplished little for God. Initially teaching at Hampton Institute, she prayed incessantly to please God, and asked for the power and ability to do her work. She had little time for non-essentials. At Christmas in 1901, having turned down a marriage proposal, she wrote: "I wonder whether I could ever love a man well enough to marry him. . . . God my Father knows all and will order all things for the best. My life belongs to Him and has been devoted to His service. . . . I know He will accept what little I have to give Him if it is genuine in sincerity of spirit." Seeking to discover God's plan for her life, House wrote:

> I mean to write down the purpose of my life, the plan by which I shall try to build up my life. . . . I am twenty-five years old and it seems to me that my purpose in life ought to be permanently fixed. . . . My purpose in life is to serve God, and to serve Him purely, seriously and gladly. The prayer of my life is that I may be pure in heart, sincere in purpose and winsome in manner.[14]

With her parents and brother still working overseas, House began considering life as an international mission worker. However, when Frances Butler died from malaria on Saint Helena, House received a call from Dr. Frissell. Feeling that it might also be a call from God, she packed her bags for Saint Helena where she joined Rossa Cooley.[15]

What were the Penn School's goals under this new leadership? Several scholars have made a powerful case that Northern liberal philanthropy in the early twentieth century sought to fashion a better rural environment in order to keep blacks and poor whites "down on the farm" and away from New England cities.[16] No doubt such ignoble intentions motivated some philanthropists. However, it seems difficult to accuse Cooley and House, who spent forty years among the African American islanders, of wanting to escape contact with poor blacks. Since Cooley and House most directly influenced Penn during the first half of the century, understanding the forces that shaped their lives and discovering their objectives for the school will best facilitate an interpretation of Penn's mission.

Cooley and House started their mission on the island with several distinct principles:

> Education no longer means to be able to read and write. . . . An educated person is one who can do something, . . . is worth something to the community, one who is fit to serve his community. . . . Penn School stands for temperance, for morality, and for Christianity. . . . The school must be Christ-like, a place where Christ will come.[17]

For Cooley and House, the Penn School meant much more than educating children. The school possessed the power to change the entire society. The workers under these new principals were more than mere teachers. House wrote, "The teachers of Penn School [are] trained negro missionaries . . . visiting the homes, helping in the Churches and Sunday schools, and teaching the children. Even more compelling than their consciously exerted influence is the quiet, unconscious power of their devoted lives of service."[18]

Cooley and House were not alone in believing that a properly operated school could alter an entire community. This was the foundational tenet of the progressive, agricultural, and industrial education movements. Despite scholarly efforts to separate them, all three were cut from the same cloth. The university professors, school teachers, clergymen, editors, and social workers who supported progressive education also endorsed industrial and agricultural education, all of which endorsed learning by doing. On Cooley's first morning teaching math, she shocked the class when she had them close their books, march outside to measure off a field, and then, utilizing geometry, sub-divide that field into sections. In science classes, Penn used the popular "Nature Study Idea" advocated by L. H. Bailey to teach students the sciences through direct observation of nature rather than through books.[19]

By focusing attention on the industrial and agricultural departments at Penn, critics have made a simple argument against the island school, suggesting that Cooley's plans undermined progress and kept the islanders "on the farm." However, this overlooks (or at least, chooses not to emphasize) two important factors.

First, while progressive education has often been praised, industrial education has been separately condemned as racist in intent. In reality, at schools like Penn these ideals lived side by side. Penn combined the best from progressive, industrial, and agricultural education, employing eight academic teachers, eight industrial teachers, one agricultural teacher, and three community workers. Cooley wrote numerous articles for both *The Southern Workman*, industrial education's chief proponent, and *Progressive Education*, the Progressive Education Association's flagship journal.

Second, Cooley certainly desired to keep the islanders on Saint Helena and away from the cities, but not to subjugate them. Cooley worked to liberate the black men from working in the factories for slave wages; she especially labored to educate the women and free them from domestic servitude in white mainland homes; and she labored to fashion a self-sufficient, progressive island community where everyone lived in equality.[20]

Penn's commitments were also significantly shaped by early twentieth-century Christian missions. Early in their careers, Cooley and House established close ties with Willis D. Weatherford, the radical Southern director for the YMCA, who often visited Saint Helena to lecture at the Penn School.[21] Weatherford propagated his ideas on racial equality and the sharing of wealth through books, magazine articles, and public meetings across the South. With his aid Penn established both a YMCA and YWCA with evangelical youth meetings twice a week. Cooley proudly wrote that the YMCA played "a most important part in the making of our boys." During the First World War, J. E. Blanton, Penn's most influential black teacher, joined Weatherford's YMCA staff ministering to African American troops in Europe.[22]

Weatherford was a prophet of the social gospel, believing there existed "a new ferment at work, a great Christian principle . . . making a vast difference in attitude" in the twentieth century. The social gospel message, with an emphasis on the improvement of society, had its forerunners in the early nineteenth century in New England Transcendentalism, Unitarianism, and Congregationalism. Furthermore, out of the evangelical Second Great Awakening in the early nineteenth century came movements for abolition, temperance, women's suffrage, and children's rights. However, the movement known as the social gospel fully emerged in the late nineteenth century and culminated prior to World War I under the leadership of such men as Washington Gladden, Charles Sheldon, and Walter Rauschenbusch. Charles Sheldon asked the crucial question which would drive the movement: "What would Jesus do?" The question was addressed not merely to one's private life but to all of society in business, industry, education, and politics. Walter Rauschenbusch was the outstanding writer of the movement, producing numerous books such as *Christianizing the Social Order* and *Christianity and the Social Crisis*. Rauschenbusch wrote one such volume for the Student Volunteer Movement and the YMCA entitled *The Social Principles of Jesus*.[23] Using this training material, students followed YMCA leaders like Willis Weatherford in preparing themselves as young missionaries "to win the world for Christ in this generation."

Penn's principals, Cooley and House, became deeply involved in Weatherford's efforts. Each summer, the YMCA sponsored a conference at Montreat, North Carolina, for southern college students, offering classes on domestic and international missions. Then in 1910, "with fear and trembling" the conference presented a seminar concerning African-American needs, and to Weatherford's "utter amazement but great delight . . . more than one-third of all the delegates enrolled in this course." With that success, the southern YMCA leadership became convinced that the time was "ripe to press a forward campaign" among college students concerning racial problems in America. Cooley and House began serving each summer on the YMCA staff, teaching classes at the student conference in North Carolina on "Negro Advancement" and "Racial Work in Rural Communities." Invited by Weatherford, Cooley and House began speaking on racial problems at conferences such as the Southern Sociological Congress in Atlanta.[24]

Inspired by this vision of social Christianity, Cooley and House labored endlessly for racial equality. One day when a white visitor at the school resisted socially meeting Penn's black teachers, the event aroused Miss House's anger:

> I lost my temper and said some brutally frank things . . . [the visitor] went to chapel with me and I introduced our teachers to her. She objected to it because I introduced them and also because I called them "Miss" and "Mr." I told her if she came over here to visit she would have to treat our teachers like ladies

and gentlemen. I also said I was very sorry if I had put her in an embarrassing position but had no idea a person who had a college training, education and culture . . . could feel that way.[25]

Like Grace House, Cooley also expressed outrage when African Americans were slighted or overlooked. Writing after World War I, she demanded an explanation as to why no African-American soldiers marched in the Paris victory parades. She pointed out that 200,000 African Americans fought in the war and several thousand died, yet none marched in the parades. She concluded her article by asking: "Must the Negro race be ignored after the record made in this world war? Their country called for men, and they responded. The color of their skin was not questioned when they were asked to give their lives for the United States. Is it impossible to grant them a place in this country where loyal service is needed from all our resident races?"[26]

Beyond its ties with Weatherford and the YMCA, Penn became connected with numerous Christian missions across the globe. As the school's programs expanded, Penn became a favorite stop-over for missionaries on furlough, many of them seeking ideas about educational reform. From Kenya to Rhodesia, from the Congo to South Africa, from Hungary to Belgium, missionaries flocked to Penn and departed with high praise for its methods. G. M. Childs from the Angola Mission wrote, "I've found in this little island a laboratory, a demonstration of the strongest and best of the great sweeping currents of the world's life . . . I only hope we may be able to do the same overseas." A South African mission worker wrote, "I found what I came to America to get—a community centre with its head in God's Heaven but with its feet firmly planted. . . . With a thousand Penns we could transform Africa."[27]

Workers from the African Methodist Episcopal Church spent "a week of inspiration" at the school. After a two-year study course at Columbia University Teachers College, Mr. Siddabingaiya from India's Education Board spent a few days at Penn before returning to his homeland. He wrote that he derived greater inspiration from his two days at Penn than in his two years in New York. African Christians traveled from their continent to Penn to learn educational methods applicable in rural African schools. In 1926, when Mabel Carney traveled through Africa studying schools for Columbia University Teachers College, she wrote Grace House, "Everywhere I go up the length and breadth of the whole continent of Africa, everyone knows of you and Miss Cooley and Penn School."[28]

Never satisfied with their labors on Saint Helena, Cooley and House believed that Penn's message "was not limited to . . . the little Sea Islands of South Carolina. It extended to all races and many countries." Like their Puritan ancestors who hoped that America could be a "shining city on a hill," for these women, Penn was God's laboratory where He would reveal His abundant life plan to all the world. Cooley wrote:

> St. Helena is well off the beaten track of travel, but . . . it is always a good plan to have the laboratory separate from the other buildings. . . . if God is using America as a great laboratory in which He will demonstrate to the rest of the world that different races can live and work together, it may be a bit of His Providence that this particular school should be so isolated a community . . . and perhaps it will be able to prove certain facts.[29]

With each passing year, Cooley and House brought a religious and revolutionary vision to the island, believing that they were building a new world. While attending a trustees' meeting, Grace House stated precisely:

> Dr. Frissell had a very clear vision for Saint Helena which I thought you [Rossa Cooley] and I, and some of the Trustees had caught, and that we were working toward a very definite goal— to bring the Kingdom of Heaven on Earth at Saint Helena.[30]

Like many social mission efforts in the early twentieth century, Penn reached for the Kingdom of God in order to bring it to earth, but the very success and cost of the abundant life often frightened Penn's board of trustees, who believed that the Penn School was being stretched to its breaking point. Cooley and House never imagined that in reaching so high they might lose their balance and fall.

5

The Abundant Life Arrives

R OSSA COOLEY AND GRACE HOUSE believed that since the dawn of time, God had always offered humanity a "more abundant life," but men and women did not always hear and receive that gift. Upon her arrival in 1904, Cooley decided that Saint Helena would receive a slice of that abundant life. A "new, full, significant gospel" would be brought to the islanders, and they would be taught to live in accordance with its precepts.[1]

However, despite the work accomplished under Laura Towne and Ellen Murray in the late nineteenth century, Saint Helena presented a serious challenge to Cooley's vision. The island remained a lonely, impoverished place, and during the first two decades of the twentieth century, many island residents decided to abandon the area seeking jobs in Savannah, Charleston, or cities in the North. During that time, Saint Helena Island lost over 2300 residents out of a population of 10,000. This community breakdown deeply concerned the islanders, especially their church leaders. Seeking to stop the exodus, African-American spiritual leaders sought to build a faith with symbolic rituals and ethics that would strengthen individual ties to the community, enable them to accept limited change, and encourage residents to remain on Saint Helena.[2] More than in the nineteenth century, the island churches and the Penn School worked closely together to establish a strong, self-supporting, abundant life community.

"The more abundant life" was a favorite New Testament phrase for Rossa Cooley. She inherited the slogan from Hollis Frissell, Hampton Institute's visionary leader, who served as the head of Penn's trustees from 1901-1917. When Frissell died in 1917, workers placed the phrase on an eight-feet-tall bas-relief marker at the Penn School. The marker reveals much about the Penn religion as Frissell stands poised with arm extended and fist clenched. One can almost hear his most often repeated message, "Struggle, struggle, struggle." With Frissell stands an African-American mechanic with wrench in hand, a Native American, and a young African-American girl. Underneath is the inscription, "The More Abundant Life Prevails."[3]

What was the "more abundant life" that God, and the Penn School, wanted to reveal to humanity? First, it meant a life that offered both opportunity and responsibility to all people and all races. Looking at the area's rural poverty, Cooley decided, "There can be a well balanced life in the country, good food and more fun, hard work and better results, houses that fit the size of the family, more cash that will bring a convenient water supply to the kitchen, a bathtub in every home, and a demand for other necessities. The Abundant life . . . is what is needed."[4]

It was in the Bible that Penn's leaders discovered God's abundant life for humanity. While the scriptures played a significant role in the lives of Penn's nineteenth-century missionaries, Cooley and House depended more completely on the Bible. For six years before coming to Penn, Rossa Cooley taught Biblical Studies at Hampton Institute. She sought to "read the Bible critically to know what to believe, devotionally to know whom to love, [and] practically to know how to live." A highly educated woman, Cooley showed familiarity and sympathy with certain aspects of Biblical higher criticism, yet maintained an orthodox theology concerning the basics of Christian faith. However, Cooley found more in her Bible than theology. She believed that the Bible contained God's plan for the reconstruction of the world and could "meet the needs of all humanity." Its precepts, if lived out faithfully, would lead to God's abundant life for the entire world.[5]

Even more than Cooley, Grace House's entire life and thought were shaped by the Christian scriptures. Born overseas as the daughter of missionaries, House filled her diaries with Biblical quotations and prayers as she sought to understand God's revelation for herself and for the world. Not satisfied to know God's general revealed will, she believed that God had given to each individual a particular work to accomplish and that this mission would be revealed to those who had ears to hear the divine whisper. Reading her Bible and praying incessantly, House awaited the heavenly call to know God's will for her life. She wrote, "I know full well that I shall be utterly unworthy of Christ's service if I look back after I once set my hand to the plough. I must give myself to the service absolutely. . . . I can only pray God to give me the strength and courage to be a worthy soldier of the cross." House was a complex character writing mystical poetry filled with great joy and deep loneliness. At times she examined her dreams, like many Biblical characters, hoping for a message from God. Ultimately, she studied the scriptures in an effort to emulate Jesus, "the man who walked the dusty roads through Galilee, the friend of sinners, the champion of the oppressed."[6]

Penn's emphasis on the Bible as God's written plan fit well with the island culture. Among the African-American islanders, the scriptures shaped every aspect of life, and biblical imagery and phrases were tightly interwoven into the fabric of the island society. Rossa Cooley wrote:

> A religious imagery overlays fields and tidal rivers. The life of the spirit walks among the Negro people. Abraham and the prophets are more real to them than the old slave owners. . . . The Biblical heroes live in the imagination of the people like the great oak on the road to Coffins Point. The big wind seems to many of them as the direct Breath of God; the thunder as God's voice. . . . Here as in few of our cities today can a speaker have confidence that every biblical allusion will be caught by his hearers.[7]

Islanders learned the scriptures through family worship, in the pray's houses at night, from the weekly Sunday sermons, in Sunday School, and during the seeking ritual. For the islanders, the Bible was "the book." An island family might possess no other literature, but a Bible was guaranteed in every home.[8]

This common base of knowledge consolidated the community by providing the islanders with a unified world vision. While other traditions, often originating in Africa, continued to operate, the biblical world view dominated. The Bible functioned not merely as a source of spiritual salvation, but as a lens through which the islanders viewed and understood their world. If an island boy saw a lion in a picture book, he asked if it were an angel. The wind was the breath of God. When a zeppelin flew over the island one day, the people pronounced it a lost angel.[9]

However, the islanders also possessed other means, outside the Bible, for discovering the abundant life plan of God. Annually, as young people entered their teen years, the "old folks" of the religious community would lead them in a ritual vision quest for God. While highly individual in nature, these rituals also attached an individual to the plantation community, and therefore strengthened the social structure of the island's abundant life.

At the turn of the century, community structure still centered around the pray's houses found on the island. Linked with the churches of the larger community, these small, local neigborhood pray's houses also possessed a life and authority of their own. Without a proper visionary experience approved by the "old folks" of the pray's house, one could never hold membership in a church or in the larger community.

In the early twentieth century, visionary experiences were common across the South in African-American religious culture, but the Sea Islands, possessing a closer link to Caribbean and African sources, practiced a more organized ritual which bound the people to the community.[10]

When many islanders were abandoning Saint Helena for jobs elsewhere, the vision quest helped link young people to the island plantations. The ritual communicated the fellowship's traditions to another generation, and brought cohesion and stability to the island. Each year, God showed faithfulness and called another generation of seekers to unite with the faith community. Furthermore, in a vicarious manner, the older members found their convictions renewed and their ties strengthened as they shared in the power of the spirit exhibited through these young visionaries. The community considered these rituals extremely serious, and seekers were relieved from other duties such as attending school, farm work, or house chores. Instead, seekers tied a white cloth around their heads and spent their time in prayer and fasting.[11]

Each summer, young people, usually thirteen to fourteen years old, ready to enter the church and feeling moved by the spirit, would spend from two days to a month seeking. What were they seeking? "Well, sir, I try to hear de Lord's voice tell me my sins are forgiven like he tell some other folks."[12] Seeking "forgiveness of sins" represented a standard evangelical practice, but the islanders' tradition involved much more. Through the ritual patterns and forms established by their community, the candidates relived the island's mythology, gained new insights about themselves, and became members of a living tradition.

In the island tradition, no salvation existed apart from the faith community. Charles Raymond, who described island religious rituals, told the story of Sarah, who experienced a traumatic two-year seeking episode. Working as his cook and separated from her African-American community, she could find no salvation even though Raymond attempted to aid her with Christian instruction. Only when she finally attended a black camp meeting did she "shout" and declare that she had been saved. Without validation from the community, salvation remained incomplete.

While revivalistic Christianity is most often associated with "individualism," Saint Helena's pattern reveals the necessity of community even in revivalism. In rites of passage, the initiate is alone and yet never entirely independent. These rites announce a person's individuality through a vivid personal experience but also remind her that she belongs to a community of people who have also passed through the same ritual. Therefore, rites of passage are times of paradox, and all communities take advantage of that paradox to integrate the individual into the fellowship and to weave group values into the individual's private psyche.[13]

Step one on the spiritual journey involved securing a spiritual guide connected with the pray's house and church. In the early 1930s, sixty percent of seekers stated that a dream or vision led them to their spiritual guide. An older friend or a church leader directed others. Rebecca Middleton, born in 1925, began seeking during her twelfth year. In a dream, she discovered that her spiritual teacher was her great-uncle, a deacon at the Orange Grove Baptist Church on the island.

Spiritual guides fulfilled many roles. They counseled the seeker by acting as a "spiritual mother" or "spiritual father," and would be addressed as such for the rest of the seeker's life. The guide acted as an intermediary between the seeker and the church. By her word alone could the seeker obtain entrance into the religious community.

As the seeker prayed, he periodically returned to the guide to whom he related his visions. The spiritual guide had received her own vision which provided a "password" by which she would know that the seeker had "come through the wilderness." Until the seeker spoke this appropriate password, the guide sent him back "to de wilderness to pray" and "catch anodder vision." Day after day, the seeker prayed and then reported the vision until he "came through."

Going into the wilderness often literally meant praying deep in the woods or in the open fields. However, the phrase could simply mean being away from other people. The wilderness could be in a graveyard, by a creek, under a tree, in a lumber yard, or in a pray's house. The primary objective was isolation in order to seek God. For Rebecca Middleton, the wilderness meant praying each day at noon, and rising in the middle of each night and walking into the yard to pray:

> When I first start praying, I get up every night and go outside.
> I afraid of the dark but my great uncle tell me to have faith. The

first night, I did not go far and I come back, but he tell me to go out farther [about a 100 yards]. After a few nights, I was not afraid. [14]

Finally, in their isolation, deprived of food and sometimes of water, the dreams and visions began to flow. Most islanders returned to their guide initially to recount visions involving the devil or attacking animals. Rebecca Middleton reported that at first she experienced bad dreams and feared that Satan lurked in the dark when she prayed at night. Other islanders perceived themselves pursued by animals, felt a hook fastened through their nostrils attempting to pull them back, or experienced dreams of dark muddy water, which signified death in the local folklore. In most cases, the vision's color scheme appeared black, and they felt that some power attempted to hold them back from getting through to God.[15]

Such visions represent a type of communication bearing many similarities to the "psychoanalytic hour." Like psychoanalysis, conversion rituals seek to construct a language describing an inner experience. Classical psychoanalytic theory states that every dream is "full of significance," and that the purpose of dreaming and dream analysis is to "stimulate . . . attentiveness in respect to . . . psychic perceptions, and to eliminate the critical spirit."[16] In that regard, the islander's visions raised to the surface deeply unconscious ideas.

Visions in which the seeker felt held back represented uncertainties on the part of the young person. Perhaps they felt unworthy to join the church or not yet ready to assume an adult role in the community. They felt uncertain about lifestyle changes that accompanied the conversion experience. One man recounted his reluctant feelings:

> When I was converted I passed through many ordeals. I was a person who did not want to give up all of the worldly things, although I wanted to be a good Christian. I loved to drink. . . . It took me three weeks to come through with my religion. If I had not been a lover of those worldly things, it would not have taken me so long. I prayed every day all day long, in a big open field. . . . When I was out there neither did I eat a thing nor drink more than a little water . . . for three weeks I ate only four pones of bread about the size of your hand. . . . I have seen many visions. This is why I believe in God more strongly.[17]

Searching for specific meanings for each individual dream symbol is unnecessary. The important point concerning these feelings of death and visions of wild animals is that during the conversion ritual young people entered a process whereby they passed from childhood into a new phase of life in the community. The dreams and visions prepared them for this new experience and social position. Dreams and visions are not merely symbols to analyze, but rather function as signs that can influence and shape people. Dreams offer a fresh viewpoint and can move people into a new life position.[18]

The spiritual guide never exhibited surprise over these evil visions; in fact, the community expected seekers to go through such fire. Some would say that "if a person has not hung over hell on a spider web that person has not been converted."[19]

Eventually, the visions would alter and seekers reported seeing God, a bright light, angels, or deceased relatives. The color scheme most often turned to a shining white as candidates recounted dreams of white horses, a shining white city, or clean white clothes.[20]

> Den I hear a voice on de odder side ob de river sayin', "Come on across, Dick, you is in de land o' promise." And de gentleman what talk to me wuz a white man and I knowed I had come t'ru.[21]

During the first decades of the twentieth century, the island community believed these visions were essential for salvation. Nothing else could take their place in revealing God to the seeker.

> All the reading in the world will not help you. Unless God opens up your understanding and reveals his mighty works to you, you are dead.
> When I was killed dead I saw the devil and the fires of hell. . . . I left hell and came out pursued by the devil. God came to me as a little man. He came in my room and said, "Come on and go with me." He was dressed in dark, but later he came dressed in white and said, "Come, and I will show you paradise. . . . " He said, "This is the living water that flows from on high." He told me to taste it. It was the best-tasting water I ever drank. . . . He carried me through all the rooms and said, "Go in peace and sin

no more. Keep fighting and look the way the lamb has gone." I said, "Thank the Lord!"[22]

When the seeker believed he had broken through to salvation, he would rush to tell his spiritual guide:

> Den I go to my spiritual mother. . . . And I bam on the door and my spiritual mother come to the door. . . . I tell 'em I dun got religion. She say, "The Lord ain't gib yo' religion. You best go back and pray some mo'." I tell 'em for true I got religion 'cause I can feel it and there ain't no use for me to pray no more. Den she say, "Well, I guess I have to let you tell 'em to de church."[23]

While most seekers required about two weeks, a few candidates experienced difficulty "getting through." Sara Singleton was born in February 1917, the granddaughter of Nancy Singleton, who in the 1860s had sailed from North Carolina to Saint Helena in a leaky boat. Sara's family farmed the eight acres purchased by Nancy in 1867. Each year the Singleton family barely survived and young Sara had little time for luxuries like the Penn School or spiritual seeking. However, nearby Scottville Baptist Church, where the Singletons attended, required membership candidates to go into the wilderness. During her fourteenth summer, Sara began seeking, with a deacon from the church serving as her spiritual guide. Sara's work interfered with the process and she required three months to "get through."

> Took me long time cause I had too many thoughts in my head. Too much work and devil wouldn't let me pray. When people left fields to eat, I went into woods to pray. One day when I left woods, the spirits come out de ground round my feet and chase me. Man tell me later not to pray in dem woods cause old grave yard out there.
> [One night while praying] De devil chase me up de dirt road. I have baby on my shoulder. De baby is you soul. I run and reach road. A man meet me and tell me that I only had another mile to go.

After three months, Sara experienced a vision in which a letter proclaimed that she was forgiven. She then saw angels baptizing her in the river and she emphasized that this was her true baptism even though the Scottville Baptist minister later performed the baptism ritual. The angels also gave her a "travel gown," a garment worn to heaven. She said it was the most beautiful robe, and the angels instructed her that sewn into the gown's back were two tickets which she must present at the window to heaven. Without a ticket, no one could enter heaven. After this she said that she got "happy," and reported these visions to her guide who knew she had religion.[24]

After the wilderness experience, the spiritual guide presented the seeker to the pray's house and then to the church where he or she would be questioned. Upon successful completion, candidates were baptized in a tidal river, always during the outgoing tide so that the person's sins were washed out to sea. Having completed this ancient ritual of seeking, inherited from Africa and packed with evangelical meanings, the seeker emerged from the water a full member, linked with the life of the larger community.

Similar ecstatic, Christian rituals had occurred on Saint Helena for over one hundred years. Traditional African rites akin to these extended back to the late 1600s. All were in an effort to bring the individual into contact with a larger, more significant existence. Nevertheless, by the early twentieth century, under the influence of the Penn School, the meaning of conversion and the vision of community life was about to change.

Cooley and House believed firmly in the need for conversion, but transformation to God's abundant life required not ecstatic dreams, but education. A Penn education was a spiritual conversion, aimed not simply at how to make a living, but at learning how to live a proper life. Preaching in the Penn chapel, Cooley explained, "The object of all true education is to give vision, purpose and power to our lives. God gives us all life. Shall we make it mere existence? Or shall we put purpose and power behind it so it shall lead to noble achievement?" A writer for Hampton's *Southern Workman* wrote of Penn, "The chief end of industrial schools . . . is the development of character. The real industrial school . . . would be better described as an institution training for social service . . . to win the world for Christ." Critics of industrial education have always misunderstood this crucial point. Industrial education was not designed to prepare workers for industrial plants. Industrial education, like progressive and agricultural education, was designed to build industry, meaning character values, into students.[25]

More than any other character value, community cooperation ranked high on the Penn School agenda and revealed the marks of true conversion. The word "service" came to Cooley's lips as often as the phrase "abundant life," the former leading to the latter.

A high percentage of Penn graduates who attended college at Hampton returned to the Carolina coast where they took jobs as teachers or community workers. They made significantly less money than they could have elsewhere, but Cooley believed that such self-sacrifice was not too much to expect from a Penn School graduate. One young graduate from Penn and Hampton was already working on a job, making $40 *a week*, when Cooley wrote to him asking him to teach at an outlying island public school in desperate need of a teacher where the salary was $35 *per month*. Understanding this as a test of the Penn spirit, the young man wrote an immediate reply, "I will start on Tuesday." Cooley made great demands on all her teachers, stating that "No one need apply for rural work who makes mental reservations as to his time and personal interests. One's whole life has to enter the community life."[26]

A major goal for Rockefeller's General Education Board (which helped to fund Penn and other rural schools) was to create independent farmers living a life of "economic individualism." However, Cooley and House centered their primary message around the community over the individual. Rather than a "rugged individualism," Penn engendered a "soft individualism" by teaching servanthood and cooperative values while simultaneously holding sacred the particular person. They idealistically believed that "individualism in the sense of isolated endeavor is becoming less and less prevalent . . . giving way to cooperation." Grace House wrote:

> The aim of life is service
> and the joy of life is love.
> The crown of life is living
> Like the One who lives above.[27]

Through "the Spirit of Service," which Cooley named explicitly as the "Spirit of Christ," Penn's teachers were determined to create "fertile fields, happy homes and noble ideals of life and living" on Saint Helena Island. Cooley wrote that if "the despised word *service* would . . . take its place above that strong word *salary*," it would "lead to a far more satisfying [life] . . . and a far greater happiness."[28]

From the moment Cooley arrived on the island, she preached and lived servanthood. She wrote that community service was no extracurricular activity, but displayed the "epitome of the new school revolution" upon which Penn had embarked. During her first year, when she discovered an old woman living in a dilapidated shack, the carpentry class moved from the school and into the community as the Penn boys built the woman a new house. Two days after the old woman moved into the house, her old shack collapsed, leaving everyone feeling that God truly worked through the Penn School. The new homeowner told Cooley:

> I t'aw't I wuz goin' to dead. But de Lord, he put me in dat house dis day. . . . Quick as dey tek me out ob dat ole house, hit fall! God is a feelin' God. He feels. He wuz just waitin' to git help![29]

If God was waiting for help to convert the world to the abundant life, Cooley determined that Penn School would provide that cooperative assistance.

Penn's community message resonated with other ideals much in vogue in the early twentieth century, especially the progressive education agenda as taught by John Dewey at Columbia University. Grace House had studied at Columbia's Teachers College, and for many years Penn had close contact with Mabel Carney, a prominant professor at Columbia, who in missionary fashion carried her progressive education ideals across Africa. John Dewey was the nation's most compelling voice proclaiming that the school could change the world. Dewey's words perfectly stated Penn's basic goals:

> When the school introduces and trains each child of society into membership within such a little community, saturating him with the spirit of service, and providing him with the instruments of effective self-direction, we shall have the deepest and best guarantee of a larger society which is worthy, lovely, and harmonious.[30]

Penn's "abundant life" community was a Christian vision of Dewey's secular "larger society." Like Dewey, Penn's leaders envisioned "a country community of home-owners living in simple attractive cottages" where beauty and comfort is found in the "flowering shrubs and gay flower gardens . . . where the well-ordered farm fields speak of industry and thrift," where schools, churches, and public buildings "point to a progressive, public-spirited people who have learned to cooperate."

More than merely teaching these ideals in the classroom, Cooley and House carried their gospel into the island community. Penn sponsored a

"Better Homes Campaign" in connection with "The National Better Homes Campaign" seeking to improve domestic living conditions in rural America. Many islanders lived in squalid conditions, but Grace House, working with seven committee members, labored tirelessly to create a demonstration house where the islanders could view a "better home," and then encouraged them to improve their own homes. That first year, with 961 communities across the nation participating, Saint Helena won third place and a $50 prize in the national campaign. Soon "a better home" was on everyone's lips. Catching the spirit of the Penn gospel, one islander proclaimed:

> I am goin to have a home. . . . A better home, yes, a better home and I am going to see that I have my windows washed, walls papered and floors scrubbed and old tin cans buried, and my wood pile in the back yard, horse stable cleaned out and a lawn and plenty of flowers planted.

The next year, by turning a ramshackle cottage into a model home, Saint Helena won second prize. In the coming years, the island continued to win national prizes for its efforts in community improvement. Penn even built a miniature version "better home," placed it on a truck and carried it about the island for everyone to see.[31]

Cooley and House were thrilled by the economic improvements sponsored by the school but, unlike Dewey's secular "larger society," Penn's efforts were means to spiritual ends. In the abundant life religion, all of life was cut from one seamless piece of cloth. Better homes meant better, more noble lives, and servanthood to the community meant serving God. Engaged in similar work across the South, W. D. Weatherford expressed their creed very well: "The neater and cleaner house means a greater interest in the home, a better home life, more care for the children, and consequently, better morals and a higher type of citizenship." Sometimes Penn's teachers wondered if the islanders understood that better homes and service to the community was connected to worshipping Jesus Christ. At least a few islanders understood. One Easter, an island woman pleased Rossa Cooley immensely, telling her, "I had the yard clean up very nice and in the house very nice to meet the great Easter morning." Cooley wrote that this demonstrated the fundamental reality which the school wanted to impart to the people. A better home life was the sanctified life of the Easter message.[32]

As Cooley and House sought to teach "hard work and better results," a cultural battle occurred over the power of the Penn School message. The islanders enjoyed Penn teaching their children to read and write, but resented efforts to alter their farming techniques and homelife. International Christian missionaries have discovered that converts often develop "a dual allegiance: a loyalty to Christianity to handle certain needs paralleled by a continuing loyalty to traditional religious practitioners to handle their power needs." From its founding, Penn faced this phenomenon. While accomplishing much during the late nineteenth century, Laura Towne and Ellen Murray resigned themselves to having little influence over certain aspects of the island culture. In contrast, Rossa Cooley never possessed any resignations because she firmly believed that God's revealed "abundant life" encompassed all of culture and struck at the "roots of the community life."[33]

Attempting to change the island culture, Penn's leaders utilized a diverse range of rituals in conveying its abundant life gospel. Each year, Penn sponsored a Farmers' Conference, which became a significant annual ritual, demonstrating the power of the Penn School message. In 1902, P. W. Dawkins initiated the first Farmers' Conference on Saint Helena to organize farm life. At that time, most islanders struggled economically, feeling locked into cotton production, persuaded by local store-owners and a long Sea Island history that cotton was the only cash crop. Yet, the islanders made little cash. Their lives seemed a "never ending circle" of borrowing money to plant, selling for little profit, and borrowing again for next year's crop.[34]

In 1909, Seaman Knapp, the nation's architect of scientific farming, visited the island. Throughout the nation, Knapp preached scientific farming, and with assistance from the Department of Agriculture and the General Education Board, established "demonstration farms" to display the greater power of progressive farming. That autumn, Knapp lectured at Penn's Farmers' Conference, and naturally, Penn School became a demonstration farm. Mr. Blanton, a teacher at Penn, became the first African-American Demonstration Agent for scientific, progressive farming methods. The cultural battle moved into full swing, and the yearly Farmers' Conference became a ritual, ceremonial event designed to demonstrate not merely better farming but the superior power of the Penn message to create a more abundant life. Seaman Knapp wrote:

> You might think that the object of our work is to increase a
> farmer's income, to teach him to double his crop . . . but if you

stop there and think that is the sole object of our work you have not seen the whole of it. There is a higher mission.[35]

The higher mission was the abundant life. In teaching that higher mission, Blanton encountered much resistance from the island farmers. They resented his advice, his walks through their fields, and his insistence that they change old farming habits. That first year, few answered Penn's call. Only six farmers felt valiant enough to trust the "progressive methods," and these men only agreed to half an acre each on their land.

Fortunately, two of the six were local Baptist ministers. Cooley believed that, "Economics and religion go hand in hand," and therefore, Penn's teachers carried their plan to the island's church leaders. Rev. D. C. Washington and Rev. Paris Simmons from Brick Baptist and Ebenezer Baptist, respectively, agreed to try Penn's formula on their farms. That summer, Cooley remarked, "their half acres were watched with trembling interest by all." When the new methods proved successful, an enthusiastic wave swept the island. Rev. Washington raised fifty-four bushels of corn on an acre compared to the island average of seventeen. Rev. Simmons doubled his crop from the previous year. Sunday morning sermons soon involved messages about corn, and the six demonstration farmers proudly wore prize buttons sent from the nation's capital.

That autumn, the agricultural fair exhibited the powerful results of the Penn School's methods. One farmer declared, "I see better corn, accordin' to my eyesight, dis year dan last and dis conference must go on!" The results proved clear for all to see, and even the most conservative and doubtful farmer would not watch his neighbor produce so much more per acre without seeking the secret of his success. Within three years, over 150 farmers on Saint Helena and four nearby islands came under the influence of Penn's progressive farm work.[36] With such remarkable success, Cooley and House began a full-scale cultural battle to convert the island to the abundant, cooperative life.

J. E. Blanton, an African-American teacher at Penn, launched one of the most significant developments with his organization of the Saint Helena Cooperative Society. The society educated farmers about new agricultural methods, made financial loans through the Saint Helena Credit Union, the first formed in South Carolina, and established cooperative buying and selling. In addition, the society's members modeled community service by undertaking public work projects avoided by others, and thus, taught the islanders to bear each others burdens in all areas of life.[37]

While heavily influenced by Penn, these cooperative efforts had roots in the native island culture and in older African traditions. African American fraternal associations existed in South Carolina as early as 1790, providing emotional and financial support during sickness and death. Poor white Carolinians also formed such societies but the organizations always held more popularity in black communities.[38] The advent of the Saint Helena Cooperative Society represented a marriage of older, African ideals with Penn's progressive communal agenda.

The cooperative society's original membership sheds light on the fusing of the two traditions. J. E. Blanton led the effort. Blanton came to Penn in 1906, an African American sent from Hampton Institute which was the nation's consummate black Christian college. Dedicated both to his race and Penn's servanthood-abundant life philosophy, Blanton's leadership in all the mutual aid programs proved vital. Another key leader, Dr. York Bailey, joined the original cooperative society in 1912. Bailey, an African-American native of the island, graduated from the Penn School and pursued his medical training at Howard University, another missionary-founded school for African Americans. He returned to Saint Helena to serve his community for the rest of his life. He always worked to bring opportunities to his fellow islanders, believing firmly both in his people and in the Penn faith. Two island ministers also joined the cooperative team from its beginning. Rev. D. C. Washington at Ebenezer Baptist Church and Rev. Paris Simmons from Brick Baptist Church led their congregations toward embracing the mutual aid message. Two Baptist deacons—Daniel Freeman and Robert Graves—also assisted in ushering in the movement.[39] These men straddled the ditch that separated the island's African-American culture and the Penn missionary tradition. With one foot in each world, they helped bridge the gap and pull the two sides together.

Following a hurricane in 1911, the Penn School and the Cooperative Society raised funds to repair 234 homes, distributed food rations and medical relief to hundreds, and provided paid work for two hundred islanders. Furthermore, the hurricane had severely damaged the island roads, providing an opportunity, in Cooley's mind, for community cooperation. The county provided oyster shells for road repair, but the islanders refused to work on the roads. Being everyone's responsibility made it no one's responsibility. Finally, the Cooperative Society decided to organize the road repairs. Less than half the island's men actually volunteered for the service but when they completed the task many new members applied for membership in the Cooperative Society.[40] Penn's religion of service was spreading.

While the road work had proved difficult to organize, it did not compare with "ditching." In a sea island environment, regular ditch digging and repairs to old ditches were necessary in order to drain water from fields. Excess standing water lowered crop production and raised mosquito reproduction. In antebellum days, ditching was a regular part of slave labor and, therefore, in the post-war era, all the more repugnant to the islanders. No one wanted to dig ditches. Moreover, if a farmer ditched on his land but his neighbor did not, it served no purpose because all the ditches were connected. Also the major arteries that seemed to belong to nobody, and into which all the small ditches ran, had collapsed from total neglect.

From the earliest years, the Farmers' Conferences advocated ditching but to no avail. The more Penn pushed, the more the farmers resisted. Finally, the Cooperative Society organized an effort to dig ditches. A battle raged all that year as many refused to participate. Neighbors argued over who was responsible for the main arteries. Despite a long, hot summer of work, when the Farmers' Fair arrived, no one could deny the results. The islanders had dug twenty-eight miles of ditches. Malaria cases dropped and crop production rose. The Penn way had again proven successful. One old farmer who had particularly opposed the ditching efforts until forced by his neighbors, spoke at the fair about his success:

> He told how he had been able to pay his debt of $200 on his house, $90 at the store . . . and then put some money in the bank. It had been a good year for him. But not a word did he say about the ditches. . . . As he walked down the aisle, someone in the audience called out, "What about those ditches?" He paused before he said, "Dem ditches ain't do one bit of harm to my lan."[41]

Penn advocated ditching, proper crop rotations, scientific fertilizing, and a host of other ideas seeking to make the best use of the land. But more than merely using the land, Cooley and House proved far ahead of their time, emphasizing environmental conservation on the islands. To replace "a great number of trees . . . recklessly destroyed by chipping," Grace House "organized a tree-planting competition" led by the Public Service Committee of students at the school. Rossa Cooley wrote, "This is God's Earth, not ours. All we have belongs to him. The Earth is Holy. Though we can subdue the Earth and have dominion over it, we must replenish it. We are . . . to use and conserve all the riches and beauty and utility of the Earth."[42]

Time and again, Penn proved the power of its doctrines to improve life on the islands. Nevertheless, farmers continued to resist efforts to change the one central feature of their lives: cotton. Cooley and House realized early in their tenure that cotton was doomed, having heard reports concerning the boll weevil far in advance of its arrival on the east coast. Each year, Penn pushed hard for crop diversification but few would listen. The summer of 1919 spelled disaster for Saint Helena—three-fourths of the crop was lost to the small worm that arrived that year. Due to its lengthy maturation period, the luxurious long-staple Sea Island cotton proved especially vulnerable. A long history ended that summer. James Johnson, an island cotton grower, spoke at the Farmers' Fair that year:

> De las' time I talk fr'm dis platform, I talk 'bout Mr. Cotton, but
> dis time I'm goin' to talk 'bout provision. I raise good cotton, . . .
> but cotton ain't stan' no mo', an' I say, "Look yuh! Wut yo' goin'
> to do 'bout de animal an' de chillun?"

From that moment in 1919, the Penn School seemed prophetic in the islanders' eyes for the teachers had long warned them about the doomed cotton. Penn's prestige soared. It had won a significant cultural war, and had proven the power of its message.[43] In the coming years, the islanders increasingly turned to Penn with their problems, and Cooley and House held tremendous influence over every aspect of life. Educational efforts increased with the start of a year-round school and a required boarding school for seniors preparing for college. Home improvement campaigns increased. If an unwed girl became pregnant, Cooley discovered the baby's father, and the boy supported the child.[44] Penn organized "Baby Days" to teach young mothers about child care and nutrition. It sponsored sanitation campaigns to encourage the building of outhouses. The school brought doctors, nurses and medicines to the people. All good things seemed to come from Penn.

6

The Faith of an Island

W HILE CERTAINLY ALTERING the island culture with the Penn message, Cooley and House also respected and embraced much island tradition. The original Yankee missionaries in the 1860s found the island rituals barbaric, but Cooley wrote that in the "praise houses is found the simplest, the most real form of the Christian religion I have ever seen." Under Cooley and House, no new plan or policy at Penn was ever adopted before it had been aired in the churches.[1] The two teachers respected the island traditions and this gained them a hearing for their Christian faith so central to the life of the Penn School.

The dramatic social accomplishments of Penn have often overshadowed the quiet reality of its spirituality. In reality, Christianity dominated the scene on the Penn campus. Every morning the two women led a prayer service at the school. Each day at noon, Penn held chapel services for students, and on Wednesdays, special speakers presided and the entire community was invited. For six years prior to her work on Saint Helena, Cooley had taught Biblical studies at Hampton Institute in Virginia. At Penn, she and Grace House taught daily Bible classes to the students, led weekly Bible studies for the island women, and held evening vesper services for the many visitors who frequented the school.[2] Penn was awash in religion, its every move shaped by faith, proclaiming God's message of the abundant life through servanthood.

Penn's emphasis on faith harmonized with a Gullah island culture utterly influenced by Christianity. In the early twentieth century, the church continued to exert a strong influence over the islanders' lives, always seeking to bind people to one another and to the island. One means of solidarity that has fascinated observers was the legal system operated by the church and pray's houses. During these years, Saint Helena was extraordinarily free from crime. No sheriff was ever stationed on the island. Instead, there existed "the powerful authority of the church in governing conduct." When any dispute arose, rather than calling for the "world's law," local pray's houses served as courts of "just law," solving grievances and crimes without relying on the county's official legal system. A woman on the island said:

> Being a part of the church meant a lot to the people on this island . . . if something went wrong between individuals, the leader of the ward [a deacon] would pick it up and bring it to the church. And, they would have a conference and talk with the individuals so they could straighten out differences . . . this informal system held this society together.[3]

The church held the authority to discipline its members, and because of the tight community structure and intense belief in the gospel, only a few cases ever went to county officials. Following Saint Paul's command in 1 Corinthians 6:1-6, islanders rarely sought outside legal council. Instead, offenders paid for stolen property, offered services to show contrition, perhaps simply apologized to restore civility, always with an eye on maintaining a communal order.[4]

Following Penn's success in so many areas of life, the island churches began to work closely in partnership with the Penn School, leading the fight to improve living conditions on the island. Brick Baptist and Ebenezer Baptist, the oldest and largest churches on the island, represented almost a quarter of the island's population. Both were located adjacent to the Penn School property, and their leadership in particular joined with Penn's staff in order to wage war on poverty, disease, unsanitary living conditions, and ignorance. This campaign represented a significant shift in faith.

Immediately after the Civil War, Christian faithfulness meant never questioning God, accepting life as it was, even holding a fatalistic attitude about poverty or sickness. Most islanders owned one pot and one frying pan per house, used long oyster shells as spoons with which to eat, and at night slept on small bunks while children lay on rags spread on the floor. Nevertheless, despite their hardships, many people feared change. Concerning disease, islanders felt helpless. The older church tradition taught that "If de Lord will you hab tarrify fever, you goin' to hab de tarrify fever. If he will you goin' to die—you a-goin' to die."[5]

In the twentieth century, new, less fatalistic, ideas emanated from the church pulpits. When typhoid broke out in 1914, many voices arose stating that the fever descended as God's just punishment for sin and any efforts to resist were against God's purposes. However, the island's pulpits supported Penn's efforts to fight the fever. When Dr. F. M. Routh from the South Carolina Board of Health arrived for two weeks to inoculate the residents, the churches and the Penn School started a crusade encouraging islanders to build sanitary outhouses and to dig new wells. Church leaders preached health issues all through the campaign which Cooley ran like a military attack, displaying an island map filled with red, yellow, and blue push pins indicating where families had built outhouses (yellow), dug wells (blue), and received inoculations (red). Working together, the churches and Penn fundamentally altered how the islanders viewed the world and how they understood God. Fatalism turned to activism, and this new type of Christian faith enabled islanders to discover a better quality of life. One islander stated, "We must stop excusing ourselves by saying the Lord sends the rain! The Lord gives us brain and strong arms for ditching [to stop flooding]. We say the Lord send the drought! He gives us brains and strong arms to save every drop of moisture by cultivating right."[6]

In many ways, religious leaders began to re-evaluate their message and rites. Between the two World Wars, conversion rituals became less dramatic and more institutionalized. An earlier faith had stressed that the true Christian was one who had hung over the fires of hell and emerged with an ecstatic, emotion-filled vision of God. The new Christianity stressed education, hard work, and community cooperation as signs of the true convert. These shifts strengthened ties to the organized church while weakening the older visionary rituals of the pray's houses.

Especially among the younger generation, there was a move toward more organized religion. While older seekers continued to pray outside, literally in the wilderness, younger seekers, especially students from the Penn School, moved indoors. In the mid-1930s, teens and adults seeking church membership were surveyed. Eighty-three percent of the younger generation reported praying indoors and forty-three percent primarily prayed in a church or a pray's house. Among the older group, only thirteen percent prayed indoors; no adult seekers reported praying in a church.[7]

In acquiring a spiritual guide, older seekers continued to be directed by "the Spirit in a dream or vision." However, only half of the school-age seekers reported such an experience. The others received instructions about locating a spiritual guide from a pastor, deacon, or other authority figure in the church. No older seekers fit into this organized church model.

Although younger seekers continued to say that they must "go into the wilderness," the meaning of these words changed. New, more organized forms emerged for discovering God. A local Methodist church began offering a class for seekers, and both Baptist and Methodist children attended. The class met for four days and an elderly woman taught the young people. The black Methodist pastor visited the class one day and stressed salvation by faith in Christ. However, during the four days, no leader encouraged a visionary experience nor did any student report one. The pastor told the young people:

> Salvation is not dependent upon doing all kinds of things and seeing all kinds of visions. Nowdays we are intelligent, and we know now, you don't have to lie down and kick the side of the house down to be saved; you just have to believe on Jesus.[8]

Countless cultural factors effected this religious evolution and new pastoral leadership was among the primary components. At the beginning of the century, almost all the area's black ministers were local men trained in the pray's houses. By 1930, in a growing number of island churches, African-American pastors arrived from the outside world, and many, even while preaching on Saint Helena each Sunday, did not reside on the island during weekdays. The Methodist church, with its non-congregational polity and higher educational standards for its pastors, underwent this change first. The presiding elders sent by the Methodist conference were rarely native islanders and almost all had at least some training at a theological school.[9] Soon, island Baptist churches, especially Brick Baptist Church, the oldest and most prominent on the island, and most receptive to Penn's message, looked beyond the island for spiritual leadership.

In 1933, Rev. Edwin Johnson arrived to pastor Brick Baptist Church. Johnson, an educated man, taught that one came to Christ by faith alone, not by visions. Such statements might have failed except Johnson supported his theology with scripture. He taught that when Jesus journeyed into the wilderness, he had already been baptized and had already received the Holy Spirit. Christ's work in the wilderness did not represent salvation but sanctification. The wilderness journey was not a prelude to pardon but represented good works after redemption.[10]

Johnson's teaching had a revolutionary effect at Brick Baptist and soon other island churches began to listen. A conflict emerged between the island's oldest beliefs represented by the pray's houses and the new ways advocated by a formally educated church leadership. The visionary seeking ritual continued on the island throughout the period prior to World War II, but it received less attention in the institutional religion. Many islanders, especially local pray's house leaders, still felt that the wilderness experience was essential for salvation, but church leaders de-emphasized it. In the nineteenth century, candidates for church membership always recounted their visions as evidence of their salvation, but by the late 1930s, baptism examiners in the church no longer inquired about visionary experiences even if the candidates had participated in a vision quest led by a pray's house guide. A fissure had appeared between the churches and pray's houses.

Emory Campbell, a Sea Island native and Penn's present director, states that as new ideas infiltrated the islands, many young African Americans simply would not participate in the old rituals. Campbell himself waited twenty-five years to join the church because he refused to partake in the ecstatic rites common in his church.[11]

During this period, a description of what it meant to be a Christian mingled both the old and the new ideas. Many young people, when questioned about their motivations for seeking God, responded with such traditional answers as, "so he will take me home when I die." Yet others expressed ideas that reflected a new set of ethics on the island: "so I can serve," or "I am going to do something he wants me to do."[12]

As new ideals mixed with the old, local island women played an especially significant role in maintaining the values of the ancient faith while propagating the teachings of the modern. Often, more than the ordained clergy, island women functioned as the primary storytellers and held responsibility for transmitting, maintaining and perpetuating the inherited Gullah culture.[13] Within the pray's houses, women had always served as spiritual teachers for seekers on a vision quest. They provided interpretations for dreams and visions, taught the candidates doctrine, and sponsored them as new members in the church. In some pray's houses women served as leaders over the entire fellowship, arriving first to light the lamps, a symbolic act displaying how each plantation community looked to the pray's house leader to provide spiritual light. After World War I, since most of the ordained clergy lived off the island, many pray's leaders, including women, led the weeknight services, examined candidates for baptism, and questioned prodigals who wished to be restored as members. Even in fellowships where men presided, women had equal opportunity to speak or pray. When women prayed, the men demonstrated their support with exclamations, "Amen, sister, dat's de trut."[14]

Yet the island women also stood on the cutting edge of the new brand of faith. When Penn leaders Cooley and House initiated their program to improve island conditions, many women immediately responded with enthusiasm. After Penn started its new curriculum, island women begged for the privilege of "comin' to school fer learn something." In response Cooley offered classes on hygiene, nutrition, and basic nursing. Longing to improve their families' lives, the women flocked to the school and demanded more.[15]

Cooley and House felt a special empathy for the island women. Cooley's book *Homes of the Freed* specifically focused on the women's needs, their hardships, their weaknesses and vulnerabilities, and the forces that oppressed them. Cooley and House wanted more for these women than mere servitude as housemaids for white families in Beaufort, Savannah, or Charleston. Instead, they hoped to help them become teachers, nurses, homemakers, mothers, farmers, and leaders in their own island communities.

A Penn cooking teacher organized Homemakers Clubs, going into the homes and teaching the women in their own kitchens. The clubs taught nutrition, canning, preserving, and pickling. One might imagine that rural people would know everything about fruits and vegetables, but prior to 1919, Saint Helena residents, locked completely into the cotton crop, grew few vegetables, and predominantly lived on grits, yams, and seafood. The Homemakers Clubs initiated a nutrition revolution. Every club meeting began with Bible devotions and prayers, and then the women launched into discussions about improving homelife with leaders listening carefully to the women's needs. No standard blueprint existed and each club created plans to fit its own members' desires. Soon the women acquired Rhode Island Red hens and a rooster, and started garden plots filled with corn, okra, beans, and tomatoes. The Homemaker Clubs completely altered the island's menu, establishing a higher standard of diet. Following the clubs' success, the women organized and led a weekly "community class" at Penn which studied the Bible, sewing, knitting, hygiene, and home nursing. Occasionally, Cooley visited and gave "talks on everything under the sun."[16]

Another area of deep concern for island women was the high infant mortality rate. Midwives with little training comforted women in labor with rituals and superstitions. Sharp objects such as an axe or hoe placed under the bed were thought to relieve labor pains. Teas made from mud dauber nests supposedly aided labor. Some women believed a baby should not be bathed for nine days after birth. The Penn school nurse started a midwives class, which met on the first Tuesday of each month. Many of these women became certified by the state as midwives, acquired uniforms, and carried their new medicine bags with great pride. As interest grew, Penn offered more extensive training to one island woman, and soon "Nurse Brisbane" became a common sight throughout the island, caring for her neighbors. The infant mortality rate dramatically dropped. Thomas Woofter from the University of North Carolina reported in 1930 that the "long and effective efforts of the island nurse had borne astounding fruits in raising the general health level."[17]

Integration of the islanders and the Penn school expanded each year, becoming more of a two-way street for sharing ideals. The twenty-three African-American teachers at Penn infiltrated the island population, gathering information about the people's needs and dreams, and they did their best to make Penn a genuine community center where everyone's ideas could be heard. The islanders felt a growing ownership toward Penn. Parents of students saw this as their school, and the ladies who flocked to the adult education program called it "we class." Penn's leaders listened and the islanders listened, and together they created a remarkable community that could survive the changes of the early twentieth century.[18]

When Cooley and House arrived on Saint Helena, many islanders were abandoning the impoverished Carolina low country, seeking better opportunities elsewhere. This fearful exodus from the island slowed after 1910. In the 1920s and 1930s, when Southerners, black and white, fled to Northern cities seeking jobs, Saint Helena islanders stayed home and worked to build their community. Throughout the island, the educational and economic situation improved. The residents caught the spirit of service and, for a magical moment, really believed that the Kingdom of God was at hand. One island woman proclaimed, "dis is de greates' day! I walk an' walk, an' yet I ain't tire. I see my limbs get lighter and lighter fo' I see de Greater Day a'comin'!"

Yet that "Greater Day" was not to be. Factors far beyond the control of the islanders or even the Penn School eroded the island's cultural foundation of isolationism. In 1930, after sixteen years of opposition by the islanders,

Beaufort County constructed a bridge linking Ladies and Saint Helena islands to the mainland.[19] World War II proved to be another link to a larger world. Following the war, young black men returned from Europe and the Pacific with a new vision for African Americans to find a place in American life. The whole fabric of American life was about to change and Saint Helena could not remain behind. The islanders would embrace the best of the emerging ideals while still clinging to a faith that had carried them through the difficult years:

> Come to we, dear Maussuh Jesus. De sun, he hot too much, de road am dat long and boggy . . . you say you gwine stand to de door and knock. But you ain't gwine stand at we door, Maussuh, and knock. We set de door plum open for yo' and watch up de road for see yo'. . . . Come Maussuh Jesus, come! We know you is near, we heart is all just tremble, we so glad for hab yo' here. And Maussuh, we church ain't good 'nuff for yo' to sit down in, but stop by de door jes' one minute, dear Maussuh Jesus, and whisper one word to we heart—one good word—we do listen, Maussuh.[20]

7

The End of the School

ROSSA COOLEY AND GRACE HOUSE retired from the Penn School in 1944. For forty years, they had labored to bring the abundant life to their students, but their influence went far beyond the annual 250 students on Penn's private school campus. By the 1930s, Penn graduates staffed almost every African-American public school in the area, altering completely the surrounding counties' educational directions, farming methods, diet, and home designs. Penn had influenced Christian missionaries across the globe, and each summer Cooley and House had toured the lecture circuit speaking about racial and religious issues. Penn seemed to be the classic success story.

Following the women's retirement, Howard Kester, a congregational minister, and his wife, Alice, arrived on Saint Helena as the new principals ready to forge a new mission on the island and use Penn as a launching pad for ministries across the South. However, in 1948 Penn accepted its last students. By 1950, the oldest African-American school in the South ceased to exist. What had happened?

Francis Cope, Jr., Penn's chairman of the board, blamed the Kesters for the school's demise. The retired Rossa Cooley simply could not understand. She asked how so many educators, missionaries, social workers, and government officials in their praise of Penn could have been wrong.[1]

The praise had been genuine. For almost ninety years, Penn had received praise from around the world. At one time, W.E.B. DuBois, the famed African-American writer and activist, applauded Penn and her sister mission schools as the "finest thing in American history." He praised the methods of character formation saying that, "It will not do in the South to leave moral training to individual homes since their homes are just recovering from the debauchery of slavery." DuBois stated that the Yankee teachers "came not to keep the Negroes in their place, but to raise them out of the defilement. . . . They founded . . . social settlements; homes where the best of the sons of the freedmen came in close and sympathetic touch with the best traditions of New England. . . . In educational power it was supreme."[2]

In 1917, the United States Bureau of Education published a report concerning black education throughout the nation. Nationally Penn School ranked extremely high, and compared with local schools in South Carolina, Penn seemed a wonder. Beaufort County public schools spent $17.76 per white child each year but only $1.61 per black child. Penn expended $70.39 per child. The average school term for white children averaged 7.5 months but only 4 months for black children. Penn operated a year-round school.

In 1927, scholars from the University of North Carolina descended on the Sea Islands to conduct an extensive cultural research project. In agreement with the Bureau of Education report, the UNC study stated that the Penn "facilities for learning are far and way above those of the other Negro rural districts of the South." In 1934, Charles Loram, graduate studies director in the Department of Race Relations at Yale, visited Penn with twelve graduate students. Loram wrote, "Our critically minded group can find nothing but praise and appreciation for Penn. . . . All are agreed that from the pedagogic point of view Penn meets their ideals more than any school they have ever seen."[3] What more could be said?

Yet the Penn School closed, and while much blame conveniently fell on the Kesters, they were not entirely at fault. Penn's collapse began at the turn of the century, the period of its ascendancy. Cooley and House, without question, won victories at Penn. They reached to heaven to bring the Kingdom of God to earth on the tiny island of Saint Helena. However, for the board of trustees, the cost of their idealism seemed staggering. Ellen Murray, who founded the Penn School in 1862, reported in December 1901 that the average monthly expenses at Penn were about $150, just under $2000 per year. By 1907, after Cooley and House had launched their dream, annual expenses rose to $10,000. In 1911, the school spent $15,516.[4] Utopian dreams are costly and the trustees began to have doubts.

In 1913, the board of trustees expressed concern over the rising costs but Cooley allayed their fears telling them about the increased work, the new buildings, and the addition of a nurse on the island. It was all for the work of God.[5]

By 1920, Penn possessed a deficit of $14,000 over operational donations and began to draw upon the school's endowment investments worth $95,000. Much anxiety occurred over the financial situation until J. P. King, the assistant treasurer, reported a record high annual donation of $39,464. For a brief time, everyone rode a wave of enthusiasm. Then came the bad news. A mistake was made in the bookkeeping. Actual donations amounted to only $16,800, and that was only the beginning of such inept accounting. George Peabody, a major Penn contributor and board member, later discovered that the treasurer's deficit estimation of $14,000 was inaccurate. Actual deficits amounted to $28,481. Several board members resigned in disgust.[6]

What response occurred at Penn in the midst of these financial crises? Cooley and House continued to reach for the dream. Immediately following the financial mistakes of the early 1920s, Cooley built the $6500 Lathers Dormitory for her boarding students and began requesting funds for a $25,000 Frissell Community House.[7] Throughout the 1920s, Penn constructed additional buildings on its campus and expanded its mission farther into the island culture.

The Great Depression crippled the agricultural South, especially places like Saint Helena, which had struggled since 1919 due to the boll weevil. During the early 1930s, the local Beaufort bank failed and soon the island lost its oyster factory, the only business on the island employing workers. Cooley estimated that eighty-seven percent of the island families had insufficient food and clothing, and she feared that many would abandon the island. In the face of these problems, Penn increased its mission to include Better Homes Programs, community classes, a library, Midwives' Class, Progressive Young Farmers, Public Health Committee, a quartet, clothing sales house, Cooperative Society, a credit union, Temperance Society, YMCA, YWCA, Girl Scouts, and Boy Scouts.[8]

In 1936, seeking additional financial support, the trustees created the Penn Sustaining Fund to stand beside the General Investment Fund. The General Education Board founded by Rockefeller contributed $42,835. With other donations, the Sustaining Fund reached $101,102 in its second year, and represented a significant victory; but expenses continued to mount. By 1941, Penn's annual expenses reached $53,178.[9] The trustees panicked.

Although the trustees worried about finances for thirty years and several resigned over the issue, in some mysterious way, Cooley completely captivated the board with her idealism. No one could tell her "no." She and

Grace House were missionaries fulfilling the work of Jesus Christ on a remote island. The board members were merely business people living comfortably in the Northeast. How could they say "no" to these women?

In private letters, board members expressed deep concern over Penn's expenses, and historians of Penn have made the financial situation a critical issue concerning its eventual closing. However, the question remains open: How significant were Penn's financial problems and were they the real cause of Penn's demise? By 1941, annual expenses were over $50,000, but Penn's investment funds continued to rise. That same year, Penn possessed stock and bond investments worth almost $238,000 and the school's total value amounted to $438,478.[10] During the thirty years (1910-1940) of financial worry over rising costs, Penn's investments consistently rose. Nevertheless, the trustees convinced themselves that Penn stood in a perpetual state of financial crisis, and this conviction contributed to the school's extinction. The problem was not lack of capital but loss of nerve.

Despite the trustees' worries, Cooley and House truly believed in their mission and in a God who would provide for their needs. In fact, Hollis Frissell, Rossa Cooley, Grace House, and George Peabody, all key leaders in the Penn endeavor, considered a large endowment to be unchristian because they believed that it implied a lack of faith in God to care for the future. Therefore, regardless of the concerns of the trustees in New York, Cooley and House with tremendous nerve, pressed forward, sacrificing their lives and all their material possessions in a forty-year work. They dreamed of God's abundant life for the African Americans of coastal Carolina and simply did not worry over finances. Cooley and House were intelligent people and knew the financial situation, and to raise funds both women spent enormous time writing letters and traveling the speaking circuit. Yet lack of funds, or the trustees' worries, never held them back. Cooley and House came from a missionary tradition that believed that if one consecrated oneself to God, then He would provide. After the two women retired, Hollingsworth Wood, chairman of the trustees, wrote a concerned letter to fellow board members that Cooley and House had spent all their personal money on Penn, leaving them nothing on which to live. Furthermore, Grace House could not ask her brother for assistance because he had spent all his life and possessions on a mission school in Greece. Wood wrote, "The whole family of Houses believes in miracles."[11]

Penn's trustees were not alone in their anxiety. Nationwide, mission schools were experiencing a loss of nerve and an identity crisis. In 1927,

Hampton Institute, Penn's guiding light, experienced a major turning point when the student body, weary of the missionary message, went on strike, and nearly 200 withdrew from the school. An article in the *Southern Workman* raised a cry of alarm from Rossa Cooley. The essay that shocked her stated that Hampton must become like other schools and its teachers like other teachers. A teaching career was "not due to consecration to a given missionary task involving the notion of personal sacrifice" but rather meant a job like any other. The Hampton writer asserted that "the missionary spirit . . . has departed. . . . In securing its teachers, Hampton must now compete on the open market and not rely on consecration."[12]

This shift arose as African Americans sought more than inspiration from education. W.E.B. DuBois withdrew his earlier praise and attacked the mission schools with their spiritual emphases. In 1930, DuBois lashed out specifically at Penn School and its supporters, raging against their misunderstanding "of what life means to these black folk, of the real difficulties of their economic and social development."[13]

In addition, African Americans wanted more control in their schools, accusing white educators of paternalism. Such accusations had substance. At the turn of the century, ninety-four missionary schools existed for African Americans, but of the 1,046 teachers employed only 370 were black (36%). The American Missionary Association, which operated seventeen secondary schools and five colleges for African Americans, had a remarkably small number, roughly 6%, of black teachers. However, regarding these issues, Penn stood above most mission schools. From 1905 until 1944, Cooley and House were the only white teachers on staff while the twenty-three others were African Americans.[14]

In response to attacks on the mission schools, other African Americans, such as educator Lewis McMillan and Howard University's Kelly Miller, came to the defense. McMillan wrote that he remembered the "great old New Englanders who wrought miracles upon and with crude Negro youths. . . . There is something bordering on holiness . . . where great men and women joined with God in man-making." The noted African-American historian E. Franklin Frazier wrote at length about this matter. Frazier admired the mission schools with their "Puritan morality," "humanity and idealism," and "virtues of industry and thrift," but he felt that with the decline of the missionary impulse and the consequent secularization of values, the black schools were altering their goals "from the making of men to the making of money." Frazier feared that students and faculty were concerned no longer with souls or their duty to society, but only with "social status and econom-ic security."[15]

From the 1920s through the mid-1940s, African-American schools, founded by Northern missionaries, altered their course, according to Miller shifting "from a Puritan to a pagan basis." Cooley fought these develop-ments, and due to the island's isolation, Penn School survived longer as a mission endeavor than most other schools. Throughout the 1930s, Cooley continued to attract her best graduates back to the islands to teach at Penn or in one of the county public schools. Nevertheless, despite Cooley's efforts, by 1940, Penn's teachers wanted something in addition to a spiritual dream.[16]

Penn and her sister schools did not decline in isolation from the larger culture. An entire age of endeavor to change the world was coming to an end. The social gospel had been fading since World War I. The influence of progressive education in America waned throughout the late 1930s, and in 1955, the Progressive Education Association folded. Times had changed. The progressive missionary movement emerged in a day when optimistic Christian thinking was on the rise, and not surprisingly, a growing secular culture in the late 1940s and 1950s rejected its creed.[17]

When Howard Kester inherited Penn in 1944, investment funds had dropped $50,000 in the previous three years and the trustees were deeply alarmed. They held high expectations that Kester would discover new direc-tions for Penn in the post-war age. Numerous ideas took shape: adult edu-cation for war veterans, a Penn seminary to train African-American minis-ters, an expanded boarding school, and more educational preparation for city as well as rural life.[18] Despite the optimism, Kester soon faced difficul-ties as his vision clashed with Penn's trustees. By 1948, investment funds had risen, but to the board members, Penn still floundered. To save the school, the trustees asked Dr. Ira Reid, head of the sociology department at Atlanta University, to evaluate Penn and design a new program. Everyone had high hopes as they awaited Reid's report.

The blow that fell was shattering. Reid recommended "the transfer of the formal educational program of Penn School to public authorities." He stated that while the island's community had once centered around the school and the churches, a new life had now emerged.

There are at least two St. Helena Islands. One is part memory
and part myth; the other is stern reality. There are at least two

Penn schools. One is a romanticized institution located and working in a land-holding Negro community with its "praise houses," "just laws," and simple, unaffected folk. The other is a real social institution working through Northern benevolences in a rapidly changing rural South Carolina community with people caught in the eddy of that change.

Reid wrote that Penn could best serve Saint Helena as a center for community planning and improvement without the financial burden of the school. Many trustees blamed Howard Kester, who quickly resigned. Nevertheless, the weary board members, filled with regrets, moved forward to implement Reid's recommendations. The Penn School would become the Penn Community Center.[19]

Without question, during the first half of the twentieth century, Penn touched countless individual lives and taught them the lessons of the abundant life. Penn graduates long served throughout the region in numerous leadership positions, and for years remained among Beaufort County's black upper social strata, but Penn failed to launch the broader, world-wide Christian revolution of which Cooley and House dreamed. However, unknown to any of Penn's leaders, a new revolution was about to get underway. And Penn would play a crucial role.

8

Penn Center: The Little Foe of All the World, 1950–1970

J UNE 1960: IN THE FACE of much animosity, Courtney Siceloff, the Penn Center's director, entered the county courtroom to testify on behalf of an islander concerning a family matter. Siceloff's reputation preceded him. Recently the Charleston *News and Courier* had attacked Siceloff, referring to Penn as a "hotbed of communist activity." When Siceloff rose to testify, the judge quickly hissed, "Come out where everyone can see you and tell who you really are and where you really come from." Then before he could speak at all, the judge instructed Siceloff to leave the courtroom immediately.[1]

How did the supposedly benign Penn School, always supported by local newspapers and institutions, arrive at the place where such fears and accusations became the daily fare? Some would suggest that Penn made a major break with its past in order to embrace the social agenda of the civil rights movement. In reality, since its founding in 1862, Penn's leadership had always stood on the cutting edge of social progress. Furthermore, and this fact is crucially important to understand, the men and women who led Penn's new programs in the 1950s and 1960s were shaped in their youth by the old Christian social gospel of education, servanthood, and cooperation which had inspired earlier Penn leaders.[2] Missing that point completely clouds the issue, and most scholars of the civil rights movement have missed the point. While the following biographies of the key players will be time consuming, a close examination of their lives reveals that far from a break with the Christian past, Penn's understanding of the civil rights movement flowed directly from its history and the "abundant life" gospel.

By January 1950, commitment was waning for Penn's board of trustees. Following almost a century of effort, these Yankees had grown weary of Southern problems.[3] When the Penn School closed, several board members resigned. The remaining members met with a young couple eager to carry forward the Penn mission. Courtney and Elizabeth Siceloff, just married the previous month, were recommended by Ira Reid, who had written the critical report on Penn in 1948. Courtney Siceloff was born in Texas in 1922, the son of a Methodist minister. While in his teens, he became deeply involved in the "Methodist Student Movement" and attended regional and national meetings from 1939 through 1941 as president of the Texas student association. Like the YMCA and the "Student Volunteer Movement," the "Methodist Student Movement" served to educate a generation of young Christians about living a life of faith in the real world. When Siceloff left home for Southwestern Methodist College, he already considered himself a conscientious objector to war, and after attending a peace conference in 1941 hosted by the American Friends Service Committee, he transferred to the Quaker school, Haverford College. There he studied under Rufus Jones, the noted Quaker writer on spirituality and theology. With the coming of war, the army drafted Siceloff but placed him in a work camp with other conscientious objectors. The camp proved to be a powerful educational experience for Siceloff; he was surrounded by older, more mature thinkers, especially Quakers, embracing peace as a way of life. After the war, he finished his college studies and sailed to Europe to work as a missionary in refugee camps with the American Friends Service Committee.[4]

Elizabeth Taylor Siceloff was born in North Carolina. Following her studies at North Carolina State University, she worked in Atlanta with the recently established Southern Regional Council, addressing racial issues in the South. In the summer of 1949, she traveled to Finland as a missionary with the American Friends Service Committee to study the "economics of peace." On her return trip aboard a steamer, she met Courtney, and they married in December.[5] That next spring, the Penn trustees hired the couple to establish new programs for community development on Saint Helena Island. They spent the summer in Mexico on a Quaker work project, and then, with their vague instructions in hand, settled on Saint Helena that autumn.

Although many Penn trustees from the North had lost interest in Saint Helena Island, a small but growing number of progressive thinking Southerners, led by South Carolina lawyer Marion Wright, continued to serve as trustees. Wright was born in 1894 in Johnston, South Carolina.

Orphaned at age six, he worked his way through college where he was high-ly influenced by University of South Carolina president and professor Samuel Mitchell.[6]

President Samuel Mitchell arrived in South Carolina in 1909 as an enthu-siastic disciple of the social gospel and an advocate for Southern reform. Seeking the abundant life for the South, he immediately set out to relate the university to the "larger movements" of the world. He traveled tirelessly speaking at church and YMCA meetings, rallying support for a progressive university that would renew the South. Under Mitchell, enrollment at the University of South Carolina swelled; however, he met opposition from state officials when he began speaking at black churches and colleges, and when he attended the Penn School's fiftieth anniversary celebration in 1912 as the key-note speaker. When he encouraged additional financial funding for the state's black schools, South Carolina Governor Coleman Blease, rallying sup-port for "white supremacy," attacked Mitchell with a vengeance, publicly denouncing the university president as a "nigger lover." Mitchell resigned in June to become president of the Medical College of Virginia, but his four years at the University of South Carolina influenced numerous young people like Marion Wright to dream of a better world.[7]

Depressed by these events, Wright left the University of South Carolina in 1914 without earning a degree. However, two years later he returned and entered the university's law school. Graduating in 1919, Wright moved to Conway, South Carolina, where he was outspoken for the political rights of African Americans. In 1945, he became deeply involved with the Southern Regional Council.

The SRC, destined to play an important role at Penn, was established in 1944 both to respond to African-American grievances and to win support for racial equality from sympathetic white business people. Guy Johnson, a strong Penn supporter and author of the book *Folk Culture on St. Helena Island*, served as the first director of the SRC. George Mitchell, the son of uni-versity president Samuel Mitchell and close friend to Elizabeth Siceloff, next presided over the SRC as it increased efforts to renounce segregation as "a cruel and needless penalty on the human spirit."[8] The Mitchell family deeply influenced early civil rights developments. In particular, an important letter from George Mitchell, written to Elizabeth Siceloff, suggested the name of James McBride Dabbs as a potential Penn supporter.

Born May 8, 1896 in Maysville, South Carolina, Dabbs attended the University of South Carolina where, like Marion Wright, he was deeply influenced by university president Samuel Mitchell. In addition, every summer during his university career, Dabbs attended the YMCA-sponsored "Southern Student Conference" hosted by W. D. Weatherford, director of the Southern YMCA and close supporter of the Penn School. Each summer in the North Carolina mountains Dabbs heard lectures on world mission issues and Southern racial problems. In 1915, he met Grace House and Rossa Cooley, who taught each summer at the conference. Dabbs's summers with the YMCA conferences motivated him to enlist with the Student Volunteer Movement for Foreign Missions (SVM).[9] However, Dabbs never consummated his commitments with the SVM. Instead, in 1916 he entered graduate studies at Clark University in Massachusetts where he struggled with his faith, and, upon the death of his wife, declared himself an agnostic.

From 1921 to 1937 he taught English at the University of South Carolina and at Coker College in Hartsville, South Carolina. Nevertheless, Dabbs could never escape the feeling of being "haunted by God." He wrote hundreds of poems and articles wrestling with his deep sense of suffering in the world, and in 1935, he wrote about his movement "Toward Christianity." Finally the next year, Dabbs wrote an essay entitled, "Beyond Tragedy," where he embraced Jesus Christ as the God-man able to carry humanity through and beyond suffering.[10] At the age of 42, Dabbs abandoned his teaching career, feeling sick of insignificant books and ideas. He retired to his family plantation to farm and write.

During the next three decades, Dabbs wrote numerous articles and books focusing on Southern culture and Christianity, defending the region's positive qualities with great love while attacking its fatal flaws. His involvement with the Penn Center, the South Carolina Council on Human Relations, and the Southern Regional Council (elected president in 1958) angered his neighbors in Maysville, South Carolina. Nevertheless, throughout the 1950s, Dabbs and Wright worked alongside the Siceloffs to establish Penn as an interracial center.[11]

Another key player on the Sea Islands was Myles Horton from the Highlander Folk School, who first toured Saint Helena Island in 1955. Horton was born in Savannah, Tennessee, in 1905. He attended Cumberland University, but his summer work during college most significantly shaped his life. Each summer Horton worked with the YMCA teaching Bible classes to the mountain people. In those classes, he discovered the deep sufferings of a people forgotten by America. After graduation, Horton worked for one year as the state director of the Tennessee YMCA under W. D. Weatherford, the "prophet of plenty." The next year, he attended Union Theological Seminary where he studied under Reinhold Niebuhr, the theologian of a realistic social Christianity.

Finally, in 1932, Horton returned to Tennessee where he met Dr. Lillian Johnson whose labor among the mountain people during the 1920s paralleled the work accomplished by Cooley and House among the Sea Islanders. Johnson offered Horton her house and land to start a school, similar to Penn, which proved highly successful at educating the mountaineers. By 1954, the Highlander Folk School had tackled racial segregation, employing a black South Carolina school teacher named Septima Clark to lead citizenship workshops.[12]

Septima Clark, later to become one of Martin Luther King's "wisest senior staff members," was born in Charleston, South Carolina in 1898. She was educated at Avery Institute, a missionary school established, like Penn, after the Civil War. For a few years, she taught at Avery Institute and considered missionary service in Asia, but she spent most of her years in the South Carolina public school system.[13] During the 1930s, she spent her summers at Columbia Teachers College in New York studying progressive education methods, and in the early 1940s, her summer residence moved to Hampton Institute, Penn's guiding light. However, it was as president of the Charleston YWCA that Clark became embroiled in African-American voting rights issues which led to her involvement with Myles Horton.

Clark met Horton in the early 1950s and began spending her summers teaching at Highlander Folk School in Tennessee. In 1956, due to conflict over her civil rights work, she lost her job as a public school teacher and her state pension. However, she and Horton simply increased their efforts at Highlander and soon turned their attention to the Carolina Sea Islands.[14]

This remarkable cast of characters, whose lifelines connected through Christian missions, the YMCA, and other student movements, all turned their attention on Saint Helena Island in the 1950s. Working at Penn, they would create a center from which would flow a powerful movement for civil rights in America. Without understanding the past decades and organizations that shaped Penn's leaders, it is easy to misjudge their version of the civil rights movement of the 1950s and 1960s as simply a secular humanitarian effort. At times, in the heat of battle, even the men and women at Penn did not always have the theological luxury of reflecting on God's leadership in their lives, but in meditative moments, like an earlier generation, they knew the source of their inspiration.

James Dabbs, devoted president of the Penn board, believed that history was shaped by many forces: economic and political. However, for Dabbs, history was the expression, directly or indirectly, of the will of God working to create the abundant life. Dabbs asserted, "God is where fullness, completeness of life is, whether we recognize him or not."

Although agnostic throughout his young adult years, Dabbs eventually returned to his Christian roots, understanding Jesus of Nazareth as the "complete man" who offers a completion to human life, individually and corporately. Dabbs discovered Jesus not in his church, but through the New Testament. He believed the church had served as an "opiate of the people" which did not "reconcile people to God but rather, reconciled them to the evils of the world." When he examined the message of the New Testament in comparison with many churches, he discovered a gross incompatibility.[15]

South Carolina school teacher Septima Clark arrived on Saint Helena also looking to Christ to guide her life's work. She wrote:

> I hope that I have—surely I wish to possess and I do strive to attain—something of the spirit of the lowly and glorious young man of Galilee, who, as I read him and understand him and worship him, saw no color or racial lines but loved with a consuming devotion all the children of God and knew them all as his brothers.[16]

Courtney Siceloff was significantly influenced by his religious past, but in his search for a better world, he often found little time for theological reflection. His Methodist childhood in Texas left him suspicious of revivalistic Christianity, and he scrupulously avoided loud language about "being saved." Instead, the Quaker faith attracted him primarily because of its social witness and its tradition of quietly seeking the will of God.

Left alone on Saint Helena, Siceloff set aside time each day for meditation, prayer, and reading in order to seek God's guidance. Twice each year, he attended a silent retreat day sponsored by the Episcopal church in Beaufort where he and his wife attended weekly services.

"God is known in love. Loving your neighbor and acting on that love." That became the creed for Siceloff during his years at Penn. God was revealed in loving action, and Courtney and Elizabeth Siceloff found plenty of action on Saint Helena at the beginning of the 1950s.[17]

The closing of the Penn School at the end of the 1940s had opened a deep chasm of distrust between the island community and Penn's board of trustees, and the Siceloffs worked hard to bridge that gap. Nevertheless, resentments persisted between the islanders and the new Penn. None of the proposed programs attracted the community's attention, and most islanders continued to hope that the Penn School would re-open. When the islanders established a branch of the NAACP and their own Saint Helena Community Council "to carry forward the standards and ideals set by the founders of Penn School," Courtney made it clear that he wanted to listen to their ideas. Soon, two projects, the Rossa Cooley Community Clinic and the Teen Canteen, found success and the islanders warmed their hearts toward the new directors.[18]

The Siceloffs made every effort to listen to the islanders' needs. In fact, they made this a central article of their faith. God was revealed through the voice of the people. Writing about the mission at Penn, Courtney Siceloff stated:

> The individuals who carry out the mission . . . should have the concern that the projects initiated should arise out of the community. While such individuals must encourage the community in the direction it might go, yet, when a decision is made, the community should feel that it is its own. . . . The community should then assume as much responsibility as practical in implementing the decision.[19]

This attitude of appreciating the African-American voice and culture proved a decisive step. Back in 1862, the first missionaries arrived believing that the islanders were merely "ignorant savages" who needed to be Americanized. The Siceloffs, Marion Wright, and James Dabbs believed otherwise. Far from being in need of Americanization, Dabbs and Wright believed that Southern blacks would be the salvation of the region. They believed that black men and women had a life of faith needed by America. Never desiring to alter island Gullah culture, Siceloff took practical steps to preserve it. Penn launched a recording project to preserve the memories of elderly islanders who could talk about the traditional Gullah culture. As local pray's houses slipped into physical decline, Siceloff took steps to "preserve the unique but important religious services."[20]

Conversion to the Penn way still meant self-sufficiency and seeking "a new birth of freedom for humanity on Saint Helena," but Penn's new role was "to guide, not determine, the community development." The Siceloffs desired to enable islanders to discover and preserve their own way of life.

> It is our opinion that people should care for their own needs.
> . . . However, there are occasions when these needs are not being met, either from lack of organization of the people concerned or from failure of the state to assume its responsibilities. In such a case, it is most commendable that an outside group . . . should come to the aid of their fellow man until that group can meet its own needs. It does not seem wise that this aid should be given indefinitely, for an injustice will be done to those who receive as well as to those who give.[21]

Since the nineteenth century, Penn had emphasized self determination, stressing that the missionaries' program was not an ultimate goal but "intended for present use only. . . . As fast as the laborers show themselves fitted for all the privileges of citizens, they should be dismissed from the system."[22] Unfortunately, when the Siceloffs arrived, almost a century had passed and the Sea Island residents had yet to discover "all the privileges of citizens."

Like Rossa Cooley and Grace House before them, Courtney and Elizabeth Siceloff could not resist the temptation to see Penn as a base from which they could convert the world. Less than two months after their arrival on Saint Helena, the Siceloffs told the board of trustees about their desire to carry the Penn message of self-help to other nearby islands. Their efforts expanded throughout the 1950s, with Penn ultimately launching a program to study the needs of rural communities along the entire South Carolina coast. Board member Marion Wright envisioned the campaign as a "pilot project" hoping it would be used as a model for similar work across the South.[23] Once again, Penn set out to convert the world.

The Center's work camps started as a project that would allow the outside world to experience the Penn message. Beginning in 1952, Siceloff invited a group of young people from the American Friends Service Committee to spend a week working at Penn. On the island, they learned that faith meant servanthood as they painted, raked, and tore down old outbuildings. Within two years, the work camps became one of the primary missions at Penn, but unknown to the enthusiastic leaders, these camps were destined to spark a crisis.

During Easter of 1954, twenty-five college students from other parts of South Carolina spent a weekend at Penn re-building the floor of the cooperative tomato packing house and salvaging materials from an old schoolhouse for use in a new one. Friday evening, the college students shared an oyster roast and sang late into the night. On Saturday evening, they picnicked on a hillside overlooking the wide Beaufort River, and returned to that site for Sunday Easter morning worship. On first glance, one can see nothing unusual about the weekend. However, this was the first interracial camp held at Penn. Students came from South Carolina State, Benedict, and Allen Universities (all African-American schools) while others arrived from the University of South Carolina and the Citadel Military Institute.[24]

Courtney Siceloff immediately understood the conversion significance of the weekend as students lived, ate, and worked together. Charlestonian Margaret Brice, one of the participants, wrote that sharing in that weekend went "a long way toward assaulting undesirable barriers." As racial events exploded across the nation that same year, numerous young people's groups came to Penn for work camps or for meetings. Marion Wright wrote to supporters telling them that Penn was taking practical steps "toward eliminating prejudice and fear from men's lives."[25]

However, events soon took a nasty turn. In the autumn of 1957, the University of South Carolina's YMCA-YWCA chapters planned a retreat at Penn. The Charleston *News and Courier* ran a story concerning the upcoming retreat and soon the university's President Russell began receiving phone calls from the Beaufort area complaining about the supposed "interracial" retreat. Ironically, while the YMCA did plan interracial retreats at Penn, this particular one was not. Unaware of this, local citizens raised a petition at the Beaufort County office building protesting the conference. In the end, the YMCA canceled the retreat. Siceloff felt deeply depressed by the outcome of the event, but was encouraged by his friends who wrote to him from the Koinonia Community in Americus, Georgia, a Christian communal farm also heavily under fire for interracial work:

> Let us all keep the faith together during these troubled times for our nation. Do not despair or become cynical. Hold fast to the vision of peace and brotherhood under God. Let not the clamor and noise of men of ill will alarm you. The Lord God has the whole world in His hands, and His truth shall surely prevail. Stand, therefore, and having done all, stand.[26]

Following the YMCA incident, Penn increased its interracial work, and local opposition began in earnest. Despite the opposition from their white neighbors, though, Penn's leaders were committed not only to improving the lives of African Americans, but also to reaching the white community with their faith message. The Siceloffs attended an Episcopal church in Beaufort, and Courtney joined some local men's clubs in order to connect with the white community. At a time when many civil rights activists began using confrontational means for changing society, Siceloff instead lived his faith in a subversive manner, working quietly and unnoticed, modeling his ideas until others accepted a new way of living. He stated:

> I acted personally in ways not normal for Whites. It was con-
> frontational in terms of speaking and acting. But I did not seek
> to confront people. I lived my example. . . . In Quaker thought,
> there is part of God in everyone. You must respect your oppo-
> nents whatever crimes committed.[27]

Penn's leaders desired to offer a message of love and reconciliation to all people. Siceloff believed that "regardless of evil acts, there is always the possibility of redemption." At the same time, Penn's leaders were not blind to evil. Siceloff offered the Penn message to all, but "it was hard to see redemption" among his most vocal opponents. Board member James Dabbs was certain of one thing: "In this world, love needs justice to support it."[28]

The faith and ethics found at Penn slowly led the center deeper into the cultural struggle of the civil rights movement. With a team of Highlander School personnel, Myles Horton arrived at Penn in 1959 to conduct citizenship workshops. These classes, designed to register African Americans to vote, were first started early in the 1950s by Mr. Esau Jenkins aboard a bus on nearby John's Island. Jenkins, while driving islanders to work, taught them to read and write so they could vote. Charleston teacher Septima Clark joined Jenkins and transported the idea to the Highlander School in Tennessee. By the end of the decade, Horton, Clark, and Jenkins were spreading citizenship schools throughout the Sea Islands. Of the many organizations that promoted the civil rights movement, leading historians consider that these citizenship schools made the single most profound contribution.[29]

The citizenship schools served a variety of purposes during the civil rights movement. Primarily, they functioned to educate African Americans about winning the right to vote. In a broader perspective, the program helped Southern blacks gain confidence in themselves and learn the power of cooperation. Especially under leaders like Clark and Jenkins, the workshops acquired a spiritual tone. Workshop leaders added new verses to old hymns such as "We Are Climbing Jacob's Ladder." The new verses proclaimed, "We are building a better nation through this school and each voter makes us stronger," providing new meaning to being "soldiers of the cross." Esau Jenkins spoke in the familiar cadence of the black preacher and his constant message proclaimed thanksgiving to God for what was happening in the civil rights movement and in the citizenship schools. Jenkins explicitly told his audience that the best way to be a Christian and to honor the Lord was to be the best person they could be through learning to read, write, and vote.[30]

Soon the message spread into the local churches as pastors encouraged their congregations to become involved. Saint Helena's churches hosted citizenship classes and organized boycotts against the Beaufort "Piggly Wiggly" grocery store and the local "five and dime" because those stores would not employ black residents.[31]

Soon Penn sponsored a "consultation on human relations" to consider the needs of South Carolina. The conference leaders proposed plans "to increase Negro voting and political consciousness" and to host workshops to provide information on "job opportunities, education, consumer education, planned parenthood, developing leadership, developing responsible citizenship." Recognizing that ministers were "often the most influential persons of the Negro community," the committee discussed ways to open communication between black and white ministers in South Carolina, and to host schools for African-American ministers concerning "their potential role of bringing about change." Noting that women were "an untapped leadership resource," the committee asked several women's groups, such as the Negro Pan-Hellenic Council, the Council of Negro Women, and the YWCA, to "devote more efforts to human relations."[32] Events moved along at an enthusiastic pace, but, by aligning itself with the Highlander Folk School and by seeking to overturn the racist structures of South Carolina, the Penn Center had entered into dangerous waters.

On July 31, 1959, police raided the Highlander Folk School in Tennessee after a magazine article called Highlander a "communist training school." The state charged Myles Horton, Septima Clark, and the other teachers with violating state segregation laws. The Supreme Court rejected an appeal, and the school's property and Myles Horton's privately owned home were confiscated without compensation. Penn now faced accusations of communism, and the future of the citizenship schools was threatened. The time was ripe for new leadership. Early the next year, the Southern Christian Leadership Conference (SCLC), led by Dr. Martin Luther King, Jr., took over Highlander's citizenship training program, and Septima Clark joined the staff of SCLC, taking charge of these classes.[33]

Penn had already made contacts with King and the SCLC when Siceloff attended a civil rights meeting for teenagers in Columbia, South Carolina where King served as the keynote speaker. Throughout the early 1960s, Penn's leaders cultivated a deepening relationship with Dr. King, and in March 1964, the SCLC held its first staff conference at Penn to organize a series of boycotts. King spoke the first day, and the Charleston *News and Courier* attacked, calling the group "radicals under orders from communist leaders."[34] Over the next few years, Martin Luther King, Jr., and the SCLC retreated to remote Saint Helena Island five times to conduct week-long planning meetings. David Garrow, prominent civil rights historian, rates these meetings as among the most important of all the national SCLC staff gatherings because there, at the Penn Center, King presented to his staff the evolution of his thought.[35]

In September 1965, the SCLC was on Saint Helena where King's staff members found some needed rest and were entertained by folk singer Joan Baez. However, conflict arose in King's ranks concerning the new work in Chicago. Staff members had made plans for door-to-door community development work in the Chicago slums. These efforts, especially those that emphasized education, appealed to workers like Septima Clark and the staff at Penn. However, younger SCLC workers hungered for the excitement of protests and demonstrations.

This conflict at Penn was part of a growing debate in the civil rights movement. Clark often clashed with Andrew Young, and she told King that SCLC energies were being misdirected. While protests were important, she believed they served only to provide attention to the movement. She feared that the time-consuming, non-glamorous but most important work of education was being forgotten. Clark told King, "It seems as if the Citizenship Education is all mine, except when it comes time to pick up the checks . . . the work is not dramatic enough to warrant their time. . . . Direct action is so glamorous and packed with emotion that most young people prefer demonstrations over genuine education."[36]

While participating in protests and demonstrations, civil rights leaders like Septima Clark primarily believed that educational efforts and cooperation would lead to the abundant life for African Americans. Penn Center leaders like Siceloff, Dabbs, Wright, and others associated with the Southern Regional Council felt similarly. Penn and the SRC recognized the legitimacy of protests, but rejected extreme, confrontational tactics. Therefore, on the recommendation of King, the SRC became the coordinating agency for the Voters Education Project.[37]

The conflicts that arose at Penn between Septima Clark and Andrew Young were merely a microcosm of a nationwide dispute over how the civil rights movement might best proceed. While embracing the movement, Penn's leaders and friends still carried the old torch of the abundant life through education, service, and cooperation. Predominantly born early in the century (or even in the late 19th-century) and deeply influenced by a Christian social message, these older leaders rejected extreme confrontational tactics, believing cultural change would come by converting and educating hearts and minds.

Many younger leaders grew weary of this slow process. The emergence of the Student Nonviolent Coordinating Committee (SNCC) created deep tensions within the civil rights movement. Many teachers and clergy committed to educational efforts attempted to slow the students down, but SNCC pressed ahead with sit-ins and protests. During the famous 1963 March on Washington, Martin Luther King, Jr. clashed with SNCC chairman John Lewis over his extremely revolutionary rhetoric. While King spoke of a dream where blacks and whites "sit down together at the table of brotherhood," Lewis's proposed speech threatened that "the revolution is at hand. . . . We will take matters into our own hands. . . . We will march through the South, through the heart of Dixie, the way Sherman did. We shall pursue our own scorched earth policy." Lewis abandoned his proposed speech only at the last moment when King threatened not to allow him on the platform.

Like King, Penn's leaders had worked closely with SNCC on several occassions, but in 1964 Courtney Siceloff also censured their activities. He had never been completely happy with the SNCC experience at Penn, and when Gulfside Methodist Center in Mississippi announced they would no longer host SNCC due to their confrontational behavior, Penn's leaders, likewise, decided to place restrictions on SNCC activities on their campus. Penn's ideals of reconciling blacks and whites led Siceloff to avoid SNCC's combative tactics. He stated, "One thing I believe in. We all are sinners. We all fall short, even if some have fallen more than others, doesn't mean you shouldn't reach out. So that is hardly confrontational. We wanted to reach both the white and black community."[38]

In November, 1966, King and his organization returned to the Penn Center for a five-day conference. Major setbacks had hampered the SCLC during the previous year and this week at Penn proved a turning point. King delivered a powerful keynote address, "Where Do We Go from Here?" which later became the outline for a book and the basis of a philosophy that guided him for the brief remainder of his life. Again, conflict tore through the ranks when opposition arose over King's evolving ideals. Many staff members desired to focus attention only on "black rights," but King had already expanded his mind to think in terms of all humanity. King insisted that the civil rights movement taking place in America represented merely part of a worldwide revolution in human rights.

The SCLC met again at Penn for week-long retreats in May and November of 1967. Instead of backing down on the previous year's statements, King intensified his argument: "We have moved from an era of civil rights to the era of human rights." That autumn, while meeting at Penn, King launched the "Poor People's Campaign," embracing those in need regardless of their race.[39] Many SCLC staff members expressed shock. They had come on board to work for the legal rights of African Americans, but King heard the call to a larger mission of spiritually reconciling all people.

King's message in 1967 fit perfectly with the doctrines propagated by Penn's leaders. In a speech three years earlier, James Dabbs had asked the question, "What is God doing in the world now?" He responded that God's providence was leading the world "racial revolution" against "imperial control." According to Dabbs, the American civil rights movement was only part of a wider action of God to free all people throughout the world.[40] Courtney Siceloff had embraced the broadest ideals of human rights before World War II when he attended Methodist and Quaker student conferences that taught the brotherhood of all humanity. By the mid-1960s, Siceloff was already busy making Penn into an alternative work site for conscientious objectors to the Vietnam War and a training post for Peace Corp volunteers preparing for overseas work.[41] Penn's leaders enthusiastically embraced King's message and were in the process of building a retreat house especially for Dr. King's use when his life, and the civil rights movement as he envisioned it, were suddenly cut short.

Since 1862, Penn leaders had labored diligently to aid African Americans across the South, and in the 1950s they very naturally found themselves involved in civil rights efforts. However, Penn's leaders avoided militant tactics, believing that the abundant life could be found through faith, education, and cooperation. Across the nation, the civil rights movement as a whole also divided along these lines. More militant leaders seemed only able to express themselves through protest without a clear plan for progress. Penn's goals, like the goals of countless black and white clergy and teachers across the South, emerged from a faith that God was progressively working in society through education and cooperation to build the abundant life of the Kingdom of God.

Throughout the 1960s, Penn hosted countless conferences focusing on human rights and world peace. Representatives from the Southern Regional Council, the NAACP, the World Peace Foundation, the American Friends Service Committee, and numerous other organizations marched across Penn's stage. Black leaders such as Tom Barnwell and Joe McDomick joined the Penn staff in the early 1960s to enlarge Penn's "Community Development Program," which carried the message of self-help throughout the region. For a brief moment in time, Penn rode a wave of success as various philanthropic foundations financially recognized the center as a shining star in a movement for social change.

Nevertheless, despite Penn's hard work for over a century, coastal South Carolina still suffered deeply from poverty. In 1968, Dr. Donald Gatch discovered intestinal parasites among a large percentage of children in Bluffton, South Carolina, located close to Saint Helena. He testified before the South Carolina General Assembly, highlighting the intense poverty of the area. Early the next year, the *New York Times* published heartbreaking articles describing the terrible conditions along the Carolina coast. Photographs of families living in filthy huts with no plumbing shocked the nation and once again reminded them of the men and women who had once been slaves and, though set free, had been abandoned on the remote islands of the South. Encouraged by the publicity, Tom Barnwell and Joe McDomick met with the U.S. Department of Health, Education and Welfare to request financial grants to create a rural health care agency. Initially funded at $750,000, within a few years they acquired a three million dollar annual budget from federal sources.[42]

Edward Pierce had promised in 1861 that as soon as the islanders were ready, they should oversee their own lives. In 1968, numerous voices arose which demanded just that. Black leaders at Penn believed that the time had come for African Americans to operate the Center and see to their own affairs. Aware of the changes throughout the nation, the Siceloffs resigned and traveled with the American Friends Service Committee to Afghanistan where they served for two years. In the early 1970s, they moved to Atlanta, Georgia, taking positions with the Southern Regional Council. Several board members also resigned at this time and were replaced by black members. Chairman of the trustees, James Dabbs, died in 1970, only hours after completing the manuscript of his final book, *Haunted by God*.

Since the early 1950s when the trustees closed the doors on the old Penn School, the Penn Center had struggled to find a proper role on Saint Helena Island. In the midst of the civil rights movement, Penn's leaders discovered a new challenge, learned a new language, and embraced fresh ideas, transforming Penn into a regional and national center for social progress. Embracing the dream of the "Great Society," Penn's leaders moved away from words like "consecration" and "missionaries." However, they could never completely escape their past. The message of the abundant life through faith, education, and cooperation always influenced their involvement in the civil rights movement. Even though Penn's leaders were, at times, uncomfortable with their own spirituality, they had been forever shaped by it. In the words of James Dabbs, they could never escape the feeling that they were "haunted by God."

9

A S AMERICAN LEISURE TIME increased after World War II, the South Carolina Sea Islands, long forgotten by mainstream America, became a magnet, attracting tourists and resort developers. A letter written in 1950 described isolated Hilton Head Island prior to its development as a millionaire's playground:

> As there is no bridge, row boats furnish the principle transportation across the Beaufort River. . . . There are no telephones, and only those who have their own power plants have electricity. Mail is delivered three times per week. The only paved road on the island leads from the dock to the beach. . . . The others are single lane sand roads. There is no resident nurse nor doctor, but the County has a clinic once a month . . . the Hilton Head Negro population numbers about 1200. . . . The white population of the Island numbers only 25.[1]

During the 1960s and 1970s resort developers seized coastal lands by every means available and turned cheap farm plots into million-dollar resort lots. Islanders fought to save their land but rising taxes and fast-talking lawyers made efforts difficult. Mrs. Alice Wine, a Sea Island resident, described the change:

> When I was growing up, I must have seen one white man in my life. And I was so scared of that white man I never see his face. . . . But now the island is full of white people. . . . Before

then you wouldn't see no white people in six or seven months. But now, the world is nothing but white people.[2]

This flood of outsiders eroded the last remnants of Gullah culture along most of South Carolina's coast. Ironically, just as Penn's leaders began opening their eyes to how God might be revealed through African-American culture, many residents on Saint Helena lost interest in traditional Gullah ways. Commenting on the pray's houses, Sea Islander William Saunders said:

> We used to enjoy the singing and shouting. . . . That place used to be full—three nights a week. You couldn't get in that place if you be late on Sunday nights. And it was so much young people. All of a sudden it just start dying off. For one thing most of the young people started going away . . . we start to be more educated, then we start getting away from this old type of thing. We come to find out that this wasn't the type of thing we needed to help us through the world. . . . This is good, but it doesn't help your eating.

Emory Campbell, another Sea Islander speaking about Gullah culture and religion, confessed, "We use to laugh at our grandmothers." Most islanders, especially Penn graduates, wanted to become polished Americans because they "had long been disparaged for their backward ways and their funny way of talking."[3] An island people who had once believed that God personally addressed them in dreams and visions seemed no longer sure if God even spoke the Gullah language.

In response, many people felt that the demise of the island culture was no loss at all. Wealthy newcomers from the North campaigned and donated large sums to save the local sea turtle and dolphin population but little money was given for the island people. Most sociologists studying the Sea Islands worked under the assumption of a mass society model that sought integration into the larger nation-state: nonassimilated groups were merely backwards people who would eventually arrive in the modern world; and there was no value in saving such cultures.[4] Even the islanders themselves strongly felt the Gullah stigma and rushed quickly to embrace American mainstream culture.

Jonathan Green, who spent his childhood on Saint Helena and later was educated as an artist at the Art Institute of Chicago, recalls the family and communal support, the feel, texture, and color from a life that now has disappeared.[5] Green remembers that each person and family had a place in the life of the community. Each family provided a specific good or service on the island. With little cash available, on an island with no supermarket or hardware store, a simple economic structure flourished where residents sold or traded their goods at roadside stands. Green proudly recalls that his grandmother produced quilts for the community. Each person had her place in the fabric of life.

Green's painting *The Passing of Eloise* is a tribute to his grandmother and shows a line of mourners who have come to pay their last respects. While the minister stands watching, one figure leans over the coffin to give a goodbye kiss. The robed choir members stand like a band of angels which await Eloise as she passes "to the other side." Green's painting provides a look at the Gullah community structure. Funerals were important events and often were postponed for up to ten days in order for family and friends to gather from around the nation. Even though many residents had moved away, the obligation of returning to the island for such events could not be avoided. The close community of the islands supported its own during times of need.[6]

Nevertheless, this close community structure was "bulldozed away in the name of progress, condos, and fast-food."[7] In the midst of these changes, as it had many times before, Penn discovered a new mission. Following the resignation of the Siceloffs in 1969, Mr. John W. Gadson became the first African-American director of Penn. Gadson soon discovered that between 1965 and 1970, 350 acres on Saint Helena had been lost through tax sales, and he initiated programs to retain the land.[8] Gadson's efforts proved highly successful, but he felt swamped with the work, especially fund-raising. Since the decline of the civil rights movement, the Penn Center had slipped out of the spotlight and large donations from national foundations had vanished. Feeling overwhelmed, Gadson resigned.

In August 1976, with high hopes for new programs, Penn's board hired John Bluffington. Unfortunately, new programs did not materialize and within a year and a half, Bluffington had spent $200,000 of Penn's endowment. Board members were outraged and fired the director in February 1978.[9]

Penn was in danger of closing and the trustees knew they had only one more chance to find the right director. In January 1980, the board hired Mr. Emory Campbell, a Sea Island native. Taking over a community center almost devoid of funds, Campbell proved a remarkable man. He collected

$50,000 that the Peace Corps owed Penn, and then quickly made contacts with various national foundations who were highly impressed with this tall, lean man. Soon new work began at Penn, focusing on legal aid to help islanders keep their inherited land.[10]

These efforts to save the land caused a few islanders to reflect on other aspects of their history. For some years, many islanders, including Emory Campbell, felt embarrassed by the Gullah language and traditional island heritage. Most simply wanted to forget the past. However, while fighting to save the land, Campbell had a change of heart and in 1981 initiated "Heritage Days" to celebrate the island's history and culture. The event started with only a few hundred people in attendance, but with each passing year it expanded. By the early 1990s over ten thousand people arrived at Penn each year in early November to remember the island's past through music, food, storytelling, lectures, and worship. Campbell had discovered a new mission for Penn in preserving "the Sea Island history, culture and environment through serving as an . . . educational resource center."[11] The York W. Bailey Cultural Museum, named in honor of the island's first African-American doctor who had so strongly supported Penn during the Cooley-House days, was established to preserve artifacts, photographs, books, and taped oral interviews depicting the lifestyles of the Sea Islands. Penn, which in the nineteenth-century had worked so hard to overcome the Gullah language and culture, became the leading advocate to preserve that heritage.

The new focus followed a trend that emerged in African-American communities across the nation following the civil rights movement. Rather than pouring energy into national campaigns, small social movements arose to address local issues. The campaign to save the Gullah land and culture has been among the most prominent.[12]

Sociologist John Smith has suggested that the Sea Island churches did not support these efforts to preserve the Gullah culture, but Rev. Ervine Green of the Brick Baptist Church on Saint Helena has made a significant contribution. In 1978, the "American Bible Society" and "Wycliff Bible Translators" decided to translate the New Testament into the Gullah language. Green was chosen as the "stage-one" translator for the version. The project amazed many islanders who had always felt inferior about their past. Green recalled its effect: "After centuries of being made fun of, Wycliff wanted to do a Gullah Bible. It meant a new pride for the people. It was a real return to their roots."[13] For many years, few islanders had referred to their past religious experiences. No one would speak about visions, dreams, or hearing the voice of God. Everyone told them that God did not really speak to them, but with the coming of the "Gullah New Testament," they began to reclaim their faith. God indeed spoke His Word in Gullah.

Furthermore, Rev. Kenneth Doe, at Saint Joseph Baptist Church on Saint Helena, has initiated programs to preserve the island's heritage by recapturing the spirit of the old pray's houses and spirituals. Doe's great-grandfather fought as one of the island's black recruits in the Civil War, and now this pastor and his church members are battling the influences of the mainland in order to restore community cohesion on the island. Saint Joseph Baptist members are organized into "wards," small groups that serve many of the old functions of the pray's houses. In addition, Rev. Doe helped initiate a "praise service" at Penn, singing the old spirituals during the annual Heritage Days celebration.[14]

Emory Campbell recognizes the power of the local churches in the island community. He says that religion "provides discipline and order in the community, and an opportunity to love one another."[15] Rev. Ervine Green agrees and is committed to community renewal by leading his congregation to love and serve one another. He states that he has "moved beyond the civil rights movement" and can never hate another man or woman regardless of race. He teaches his congregation, "If there is to be peace someday, then I must live that peace now."

Rev. Green believes deeply in the "power of humility, servanthood, and suffering," and he certainly suffers for his people. He arrived quite late one night when he was to speak at a mission conference at Penn Center. Green had been visiting local "crack houses" searching for a teenager whose mother had phoned the church worried that her son was involved in drugs. Like many other leaders on the island, Rev. Green questions what benefits have come across the bridge from the mainland to Saint Helena.[16]

Campbell poses similar questions about contact with the mainland and an excessive dependence on outside dollars. Following in the abundant life tradition, Campbell dreams of creating "a sustainable community" that is "not dependent on the outside world." As in preceding years, Penn continues to act "as a catalyst for the development of programs for self-sufficiency," encouraging the islanders to rely on themselves, urging them to use their own goods and services rather than looking for tourist dollars as a panacea.[17] In moves highly reminiscent of Rossa Cooley and Grace House, Campbell is currently helping the islanders build a food-processing factory for local crops and seafood, and develop a cooperative community market to sell island-grown produce. Penn is also creating a twelve-week school that teaches community development. Campbell believes that the answers to Saint Helena's problems lie on the island itself, not on the mainland. Questioning the values of "progress" and "modern America," many islanders agree with him. They regret the loss of their land and cultural heritage, resent the growing drug and family problems, and feel concern about the destruction of the wetlands environment.[18]

Cooley and House have been criticized by historians for efforts in the 1920s to keep the islanders "at home" and for encouraging them to seek the abundant life by building their own communities. During those years W.E.B. DuBois attacked Penn and urged the younger generation of African-Americans to flee the South. But when the "talented tenth" followed his advice, it only served to further depress the region. Now as a new century begins, Cooley's old ideals of the abundant life seem to speak again to the Sea Islanders. Community cooperation and service are again becoming fashionable.

A final story completes the circle. Emory Campbell says, "We use to laugh at our grandmothers" because of their Gullah speech. "Now I know that Gullah was our link to Africa." In October 1988, Penn Center arranged for the President of Sierra Leone to visit and speak on Saint Helena Island. The event wrought a remarkable conversion. Many islanders, especially Penn graduates, had sought to forget their African past. However, with the coming of President Joseph Momoh, Campbell states, "The Penn graduates had an immediate change of mind about Africa." As President Momoh spoke, the islanders sat amazed as they understood every word. This man from West Africa spoke Gullah. The event brought a "new dignity to a people who had long been disparaged for their backward ways and their funny way of talking."[19] Suddenly, they knew that their grandparents did not speak a backwards, sub-standard English. They spoke African. The Gullah history and culture was valuable and worth saving.

In November 1989, Campbell and a group from Saint Helena traveled to Sierra Leone, back to West Africa, where their ancestors had been enslaved centuries ago. As they disembarked from the plane, the crowd awaiting them shouted, "Thank God, you've come home." The group toured for a week and one bright beautiful morning they sailed to Bunce Island in the middle of the Sierra Leone river where slaves had once been herded onto ships bound for South Carolina. On this island, centuries ago, their ancestors had last stood on African soil.[20]

Cornelia Bailey confessed, "We knew the purpose of going there, but the emotion didn't start until you actually got there. . . . It's hard to describe. . . . It made me angry."

Elaine Jenkins, a lawyer and the daughter of Esau Jenkins who started the first citizenship classes in the South, stated, "It's too painful. . . . Every time I think about it, I cry."

The experience moved John Matthews to deep reflections. "I really questioned human values. How can people do such things to people? . . . You had a lavish house with a lavish living style [and] twenty feet away you had people in chains eating rice out of a trough. It's inhuman."

As Earnestine Atkins walked about Bunce Island thinking of her ancestors carried away to Saint Helena Island on the opposite side of the Atlantic, she imagined "the screams in their hearts, wanting to go back to their families" but never again being able to see their home or loved ones.[21]

Campbell and his fellow travelers returned to South Carolina with a new understanding of their African heritage and a new commitment to keep that heritage alive. The United States Department of the Interior recognized the Penn Center as a National Historic Landmark District, one of only three in South Carolina, and Penn launched a campaign to renovate the old campus and to continue its work on the South Carolina Sea Islands.

Novelist John Jakes believes that "Penn Center is one of the great historic sites in America. This school, born in the era of fire and struggle . . . , stands as a major milestone on the road to freedom, equality, and education for all." Vertamae Smart-Grosvenor of National Public Radio proclaimed, "Penn Center is American history. Some of the most dramatic events in our nation's history occurred on Penn's grounds and in the region." However, Penn is more than history. Penn represents the future of the Sea Islands, serving as an advocate for the people, leading them to the abundant life. Smart-Grosvenor concluded, "Penn Center is the keeper of the culture. . . . Helping Penn Center survive is a golden opportunity to preserve and honor the past, respect the present and safeguard the future."[22]

* * * * * *

I ONCE KNEW A PLACE on the South Carolina coast where the Spanish moss hung from ancient twisted live oak trees and at night the moonlight would cast eerie shadows on the narrow roads. However, from Murrells Inlet to Hilton Head Island, the quiet places of the South Carolina coast have vanished. The waters that separated them from the mainland were not wide enough to hold back the twentieth century, and now many coastal residents worry what the twenty-first century will bring. Will the promised abundant life finally prevail? And whose vision of the abundant life will that be?

Throughout the centuries, various cultures have clashed on the Sea Islands: Spanish and French, English and Native American, slaves and plantation owners, freedmen and missionaries, islanders and resort developers. The strength of the region and its people was always through embracing the future while maintaining their heritage. Those who came proclaiming "progress" did not always best serve the interests of the islanders, but neither was the abundant life found simply by clinging to the past.

Religious motivations have powerfully influenced the residents of Saint Helena. In fact, as with all of American society, these are among the glues that hold the culture together. In American history, ignoring religion means misunderstanding history and the motivations of much social progressivism. Religion cannot be kept separate but rather is part of the whole fabric of American society. On Saint Helena Island, scholars, social workers, and educators miss the point completely if they fail to recognize the importance of religious faith. Africans brought their faith with them across the rough Atlantic. African Americans discovered in Christ a fellow traveler on the way of suffering. Penn missionaries always believed that God was at work to change the world, whether that meant classroom education, planting better corn, or marching for civil rights. Whatever direction Saint Helena takes, whatever the abundant life means for the future, religious faith will be part of that life.

In seeking that abundant life, Penn's leaders labored to make Saint Helena Island a self-sufficient society, but they did not envision the island as a completely isolated community. From Edward Pierce and Laura Towne to Rossa Cooley and Courtney Siceloff, Penn's leaders dreamed that Saint Helena would become a shining city on a hill for all the world to see: a model community which others could emulate. Working with great faith, they believed that the gospel of the abundant life would eventually prevail and bring the Kingdom of God to earth.

South Carolina's Sea Islands have experienced centuries of struggle as various cultures and peoples have come to these shores with conflicting dreams. That cultural clash continues throughout the islands: in courtrooms, in churches, in backroad crack houses, and of course, at the Penn Center. If history can provide guidance for an abundant life in the future, then the narrative of the Penn School and Saint Helena Island should be heard. Despite false promises and unfulfilled dreams, W.E.B. DuBois still said that this story was the "finest thing in American history."[23]

Notes

Notes to Preface:

[1]Pat Conroy, *The Water Is Wide* (Boston: Houghton Mifflin, 1972). Conroy taught school for one year on the Sea Islands.

[2]Margaret Washington Creel, *A Peculiar People: Slave Religion and Community Culture Among the Gullahs* (New York: New York University Press, 1988): 22.

[3]Willie Lee Rose, *Rehearsal for Reconstruction: The Port Royal Experiment* (New York: Oxford University Press, 1964).

[4]Numerous books designate the small, local worship centers on the Sea Islands as "praise houses," but the spelling "pray's house" appears in the earliest written sources. Furthermore, Samuel Lawton interviewed numerous islanders in the 1930s who explained that the "prayers house" was where they "go fur pray." The term "praise house" was merely a missionary misunderstanding, which has now become a common title. See *Southern Christian Advocate* (July 28, 1843); Samuel Miller Lawton, "The Religious Life of South Carolina Coastal and Sea Island Negroes" (Ph.D. dissertation, George Peabody College for Teachers, 1939): 55.

[5]Mary Boys, *Educating in Faith*, (Sheed and Ward, 1993): 6; Boys's work on religious education provided an excellent framework of questions for this work.

Notes to Chapter 1:

[1]Edith M. Dabbs, *Sea Island Diary* (Spartanburg, SC: Reprint Company, Publishers, 1983): 6; Guion G. Johnson, *A Social History of the Sea Islands* (New York: Negro University Press, 1969 [first published by University of North Carolina Press, 1930]): 3, 5; Herbert Aptheker, *American Negro Slave Revolts*, 2nd ed. (New York, 1969): 163. Some evidence suggests that nomadic Native Americans lived along the coast as early as 12,000 B.C. The exact location of this first Spanish colony is unknown.

[2]Jeannette T. Conner, ed., *Jean Ribaut, The Whole and True Discouerye of Terra Florida* (Florida State Historical Society, 1927): 90f; Dabbs, *Sea Island Diary*, 16-17.

[3]Stanley South, "Santa Elena: Threshold of Conquest" in *The Recovery of Meaning: Historical Archaeology in the Eastern United States*, edited by Mark P. Leone and Parker B. Potter, Jr. (Washington DC: Smithsonian Institute Press, 1988): 33-36; Chester DePratter and Stanley South, *Discovery at Santa Elena*, Research Manuscript 221 (Columbia: South Carolina Institute of Archaeology, 1995): 7-11. Stanley South, "The Search for Santa Elena on Parris Island, South Carolina," University of South Carolina, Institute of Archaeology and Anthropology, Research Manuscript Series 150: 85; Kathleen A. Deagan, "The Archaeology of Sixteenth Century St. Augustine," *The Florida Anthropologist* 38 (1-2), pt. 1: 11-12.

[4][Wofford E. Malphrus] *A History of Euhaw Baptist Church, 1686-1995* (published by the Euhaw Baptist Church in 1995; Euhaw Baptist Church Papers, Furman University Archives, Greenville, SC): 2; The "Cardross-Dunlop colony" of 1684 is an almost-unknown tale, yet it appears to be the second-oldest Baptist church in the South and played an important role in evangelizing slaves.

[5]A.S. Salley, Jr., *Warrants for Lands in South Carolina, 1692-1711* (Columbia, SC): 152; Peter H. Wood, *Black Majority* (New York: W. W. Norton & Company, 1974): 21, 131; Samuel Dyssli, December 3, 1737, *South Carolina Historical and Genealogical Magazine*, 90; Edward McGrady, *History of South Carolina Under the Royal Government, 1670-1776* (New York, 1889): 807; James W. Loewen, *Lies My Teacher Told Me* (New York: New Press, 1995): 98.

[6]Wood, *Black Majority*, 127; Katharine M. Jones, *Port Royal Under Six Flags* (New York: Bobbs-Merrill Co., 1960): 99; Transcripts of *British Public Records Office Relating to South Carolina, 1663-1782*, vol. 6, South Carolina Department of Archives and History, 107.

[7]Wood, *Black Majority*, 147; Creel, *A Peculiar People*, 70-71; Dabbs, *Sea Island Diary*, 7, 67; Abigail Capers to Eliza Russell, March 25, 1791, James McBride Dabbs Papers, Southern Historical Collection, University of North Carolina.

[8]Malphrus, *Euhaw Baptist Church*; Creel, *A Peculiar People*, 73.

[9]E. Franklin Frazier, *The Negro Church in America* (New York: Schocken Books, 1964): 1-19.

[10]Melville J. Herskovits, "The Negro in the New World: The Statement of a Problem," *American Anthropologist* 32 (1930): 149f; Melville J. Herskovits, *The Myth of the Negro Past* (Boston: Beacon Press, 1958): 77-81, 86-109.

[11]James Glen, *A Description of South Carolina* (London, 1761), republished in Chapman J. Milling, ed., *Colonial South Carolina: Two Contemporary Descriptions* (Columbia, SC, 1951): 95.

[12]Philip M. Hamer, ed., *Papers of Henry Laurens*, 4 (Columbia: University of South Carolina Press, 1968): 294-295; "Family Across the Sea," Teacher's Guide for the film (Columbia: South Carolina Educational Television, 1990).

[13]Lorenzo Turner, *Africanisms in the Gullah Dialect* (Chicago: University of Chicago Press, 1949).

[14]Elizabeth Ware Pearson, ed., *Letters from Port Royal* (Boston: W. B. Clarke, 1906; reprinted New York: Arno Press, 1969): 203 (this letter was originally published in *New York Nation*, 30 May 1867); John S. Bogert, February 17, 1865, South Carolina Historical Society Manuscripts Collection.

[15]Edward Pierce, "The Negroes at Port Royal," *The Rebellion Record*, ed. Frank Moore, Suppl. 1 (New York: Putnam & Holt, 1864): 304; John F. Szwed, "Africa Lies Just Off Georgia," *Africa Report* 15 (Oct 1970): 29; William R. Bascom, "Acculturation Among the Gullah Negroes," *American Anthropologist* 43 (1941): 43f.

[16]Thomas R. Wheaton and Patrick H. Garrow, "Acculturation and the Archaeological Record in the Carolina Lowcountry," in *The Archaeology of Slavery and Plantation Life*, ed. Theresa A. Singleton (New York: Academic Press, 1985): 242, 244-248; Michael Trinkley, *Indian and Freedmen Occupation at the Fish Haul Site, Beaufort, South Carolina* (Columbia, SC: Chicora Foundation: 1986): 130, 251.

[17]The following resources describe these African religious practices:

Creel, *A Peculiar People*, 29-63; K. L. Little, "The Poro Society as an Arbiter of Culture," *African Studies* 7 (March 1948): 1-4; K. L. Little, "The Role of the Secret Society in Cultural Specialization," *American Anthropologist* 51 (April-June 1949): 199f; Richard Fulton, "The Political Structures and Functions of Poro in Kpelle Society," *American Anthropologist* 74 (October 1972): 1218f.

[18]Frederick Dalcho, *An Historical Account of the Protestant Episcopal Church in South Carolina* (Charleston, SC: 1820); Albert S. Thomas, *A Historical Account of the Protestant Episcopal Church in South Carolina, 1820-1957* (Columbia, SC: R. L. Bryan, 1957).

[19]Dabbs, *Sea Island Diary*, 105-106.

[20]As explained earlier, the spelling "pray's house" is preferable over "praise house."

[21]W. Harrison Daniel, "Virginia Baptists and the Negro in the Early Republic," *The Virginia Magazine of History and Biography*, 80 (Richmond: Virginia Historical Society, 1972): 60.

[22]"Work among the Negroes," 9 October 1840, 8 October 1841, 8 October 1842, Minutes of the Beaufort Baptist Church, Baptist Collection, Furman University; Creel, *A Peculiar People*, 229-230.

[23]Interview with Wofford Malphrus, historian of Euhaw Baptist Church; Creel, *A Peculiar People*, 58; Dabbs, *Sea Island Diary*, 108-109; Fredrick L. Olmsted, *A Journey in the Seaboard Slaves States* (New York, 1856): 449.

[24]*Christian Advocate and Journal*,January 22, 1836, July 22, 1836; William Capers, "Missionary," *Southern Christian Advocate*, (September 29, 1843).

[25]John N. Davies, "Missions," *Southern Christian Advocate* (June 26, 1840).

[26]Charles C. Jones, *The Religious Instruction of the Negroes* (Savannah, GA: Thomas Purse, 1842): 83.

[27]Herskovits, *The Myth of the Negro Past*, 207, 232-35.

[28]Elias Bower, *Slavery in the Methodist Episcopal Church* (Auburn, AL: William J. Moses Printer, 1859): 28.

[29]Wesley M. Gewehr, *The Great Awakening in Virginia 1740-1790* (Durham, NC: Duke University Press, 1930): 243; Garnett Ryland, *The Baptists of Virginia* (Richmond: Virginia Baptist Board of Missions, 1955): 151.

[30]Louis Philippe, *Diary of My Travels in America*, translated by Stephen Becker, (New York: Delaconte Press, 1977): 31.

[31]Creel, *A Peculiar People*: 73.

[32]Albert J. Raboteau, *Slave Religion* (New York: Oxford University Press, 1978): 209-210, 239f.

[33]Wheaton and Garrow, "Acculturation in the Carolina Lowcountry," 242, 251; Theresa A. Singleton, "An Archaeological Framework for Slavery and Emancipation, 1740-1880," in Leone and Potter, *The Recovery of Meaning*, 346-347, 354f; Trinkley, *Indian and Freedmen Occupation*, 215. There are exceptions to this acculturation to the material culture. In 1908 W.E.B. DuBois described slave quarters in Florida that maintained an African architectural form. See W.E.B. DuBois, *The Negro American Family* (Westport, CT: Negro Universities Press, 1969). Archaeologist George McDaniel uncovered an African-styled slave house built in the 1850s. See George W. McDaniel, *Hearth and Home: Preserving a People's Culture* (Philadelphia: Temple University Press, 1982). However, these examples are the exception to the rule. Almost all archaeological evidence demonstrates a rapid decline in African architectural patterns after 1800.

[34]Pierce, "The Negroes at Port Royal, S.C.," 305; David Franklin Thorpe Papers, 25 January 1863, Southern Historical Collection, Wilson Library, University of North Carolina, Box 1.

[34]Donald G. Matthews, *Religion in the Old South* (Chicago: University of Chicago Press, 1977): 186f.

[36]Johnson, *A Social History of the Sea Islands*, 154; *Charleston Daily Courier*, December 2, 1861.

[37]"The Capture of Port Royal, S.C.," *Rebellion Record*, ed. Frank Moore, Supplement I (New York: Putnam and Holt, 1864): 186-193; Thomas, *Historical Account of the Protestant Episcopal Church in South Carolina*.

[38]Hazard Stevens, *The Life of Isaac Ingalls Stevens* (Boston, 1900): 354-355; *War of the Rebellion: A Compilation of the Official Records of the Union and Confederate Armies*, series 1, vol. 6, serial no. 6, (Washington DC, 1880): 202.

[39]*New York Tribune*, December 7, 1861. Samuel F. Du Pont to Henry W. Davis, February 25, 1862, Du Pont Papers, Eleutherian Mills Historical Library, Wilmington, Delaware.

[40]*New York Times*, February 24, 1862; *Ancestors and Descendants of Samuel French the Joiner* (Ann Arbor, MI: 1940).

[41]Edward Pierce to Chase, February 3, 1862, *The Rebellion Record*, 314; Rose, *Rehearsal for Reconstruction*, 27.

Notes to Chapter 2:

[1]Edward Pierce, "The Freedmen at Port Royal," *Atlantic Monthly*, 12 (September, 1863): 298-299; Rose, *Rehearsal for Reconstruction*. W. L. Rose conducted the groundbreaking research on the Port Royal missionaries of the 1860s. Though Rose is very helpful in understanding the land controversary, theological concerns are not high on her agenda.

[2]Robert N. Bellah, "Civil Religion in America," *Daedalus*, 96 (1967): 1, 5.

[3]Pierce, "The Negroes at Port Royal, S.C.," 302-304.

[4]Pierce, "The Negroes at Port Royal, S.C.," 312.

[5]Edward Pierce, *Boston Transcript*, 27 January 1862; *First Annual Report of the Boston Educational Commission for Freedmen, May 1863* (Boston, 1863): 4. This seemingly contradictory phrase, "evangelical Unitarianism," was coined by Timothy Smith in *Revivalism and Social Reform: American Protestantism on the Eve of the Civil War* (New York: Harcourt, Brace and World, 1965): 95-102. Also see Anne C. Rose, *Transcendentalism as a Social Movement, 1830-1850* (New Haven: Yale University Press, 1981): 2-37. "Evangelical Unitarianism" continued to influence Bostonians through the 1850s, including most of the young missionaries who sailed south.

[6]Smith, *Revivalism and Social Reform*, 63-79; New York National Freedmen Relief Association, *Annual Report* (New York: 1866): 8-9; *A History of the American Missionary Association* (New York, 1874): 13.

[7]Pierce, "The Freedmen at Port Royal," 298; Laura Towne, "Company of Port Royalists, April 9, 1862," Penn School Papers, Southern Historical Collection, University of North Carolina, reel 18.

[8]Rose, *Transcendentalism as a Social Movement, 1830-1850*, 2, 13; William C. Gannett, *Ezra Stiles Gannett: Unitarian Minister in Boston, 1824-1871* (Boston: Roberts Brothers, 1875); William C. Gannett, "Steamer Atlantic," William C. Gannett Papers, University of Rochester; William H. Pease, "Three Years Among the Freedmen," *Journal of Negro History*, 42 (April 1957): 98; Pearson, ed., *Letters from Port Royal, 1862-1868*, 166, 249.

[9]Pearson, ed., *Letters from Port Royal, 1862-1868*, iii, 68, 95; Ware family biographies, *The Dictionary of American Biographies*, ed. Dumas Malone (New York: Charles Scribner's Sons): 446-451; Rose, *Transcendentalism as a Social Movement, 1830-1850*, 32-33.

[10]"Biography of Laura Towne," Penn School Papers, Southern Historical Collection, University of North Carolina, reel 18; Rupert Sargent Holland, ed., *The Letters and Diary of Laura M. Towne* (New York: Negro Universities Press, 1969): 66; Ray Allen Billington, ed., *The Journal of Charlotte L. Forten* (New York: Collier Books): 10, 17, 24, 25, 29, 30, 32, 137, 138.

[11]Holland, *The Letters and Diary of Laura M. Towne*, 136; Mary M. Thorpe, 26 August 1865, David Franklin Thorpe Papers, Southern Historical Collection, Wilson Library, University of North Carolina at Chapel Hill, Box 1; Botume, *First Days Amongst the Contrabands* (Boston: Lee and Shepard Publ., 1893): 35.

[12]Kenneth Scott Latourette, *Christianity in a Revolutionary Age*, III (Grand Rapids, MI: Zondervan, 1969): 152-165; William R. Hutchison, *The Modernist Impulse in American Protestantism* (Cambridge, MA: Harvard University Press, 1976); Frank L. Baumer, "Romanticism," *The Dictionary of the History of Ideas*, Philip P. Wiener, ed. (New York: Charles Scribner's Sons, 1973): 198-204.

[13]Pearson, ed., *Letters from Port Royal, 1862-1868*, 105; Pierce, "The Freedmen at Port Royal," 299-300; T. D. Howard, "Before and After Emancipation," *Unitarian Review* (August 1888): 137.

[14]Bellah, "Civil Religion in America," 1, 5.

[15]Billington, ed., *The Journal of Charlotte L. Forten*, 150; Timothy Smith, *Revivalism and Social Reform*, 95-102; Latourette, *Christianity in a Revolutionary Age*, 154; Luther P. Jackson, "The Educational Efforts of the Freedmen's Bureau and Freedmen's Aid Societies in South Carolina, 1862-1872," *The Journal of Negro History* (January 1923): 10; Holland, ed., *The Letters and Diary of Laura M. Towne*, 172, 203, 301.

[16]Baumer, "Romanticism," 198-204; Billington, *The Journal of Charlotte L. Forten*, 139, 173. Forten emphasized that her brother gave her money specifically to purchase a copy of Hugo's book prior to her departure for South Carolina. She mentions seeing the book in the possession of other Yankee missionaries.

[17]Pierce, "The Freedmen at Port Royal," 315; Howard, "Before and After Emancipation," 144.

[18][W. C. Gannett and E. E. Hale], "The Freedmen at Port Royal," *North American Review*, 101 (July, 1865): 1, 7, 13; Jackson, "The Educational Efforts of the Freedmen's Bureau," 13; *Senate Executive Documents*, 38th Congress, First Session, vol. 1, no. 1 (Library of Congress): 2-6; Pierce, "The Freedmen at Port Royal," 315; Oliver O. Howard, *Autobiography*, vol. II (New York, 1907): 221.

[19]Richard B. Drake, "The American Missionary Association and the Southern Negro, 1861-1888" (Ph.D. dissertation, Emory University, 1957): 40, 16.

[20]Holland, ed., *The Letters and Diary of Laura M. Towne*, 63, 90; Pearson, ed., *Letters from Port Royal, 1862-1868*, 50.

[21]Horace Bushnell, *God in Christ* (Hartford: Brown and Parsons, 1849); Horace Bushnell, *Christian Nurture* (New York: Charles Scribner's Sons, 1861).

[22]Bellah, "Civil Religion in America," 11.

[23]Pierce, "The Freedmen at Port Royal," 310; Holland, ed., *The Letters and Diary of Laura M. Towne*, 133.

[24]Rose, *Transcendentalism as a Social Movement*, 29-30, The similarities of theory are remarkable between the 1830s and the 1860s. Concerning the Boston schools in the 1830s, Anne Rose wrote that the "primary objective of these groups was not economic aid, but moral improvement of the working class by personal contact with exemplary Christians." Joseph Tuckerman, William Ellery Channing, and Cyrus Bartol all wrote short manuals instructing Christians in how to be a "visitor of the poor" with the prime objective being "a greater extension of human virtue and happiness."

[25]Holland, ed., *The Letters and Diary of Laura M. Towne*, 68.

[26]Pearson, ed., *Letters from Port Royal, 1862-1868*, 241; Botume, *First Days Amongst the Contrabands*, 112.

[27]Edward Pierce, "Second Report, Port Royal, June 2, 1862," *Rebellion Record*, ed. Frank Moore, Supplement I (New York: Putnam and Holt, 1864): 321; Pierce, "The Freedmen at Port Royal," 297.

[28]Jacob Stroyer, *My Life in the South* (Salem, MA, 1898): 16.

[29]Pierce, "The Negroes at Port Royal, S.C.," 306; Botume, *First Days*

Amongst the Contrabands, 157; Holland, ed., *The Letters and Diary of Laura M. Towne*, 53; Pearson, ed., *Letters from Port Royal, 1862-1868*, 95.

[30]Pearson, ed., *Letters from Port Royal, 1862-1868*, 216, 220, 257, 296, 303.

[31]Pierce, "The Freedmen at Port Royal," 298.

[32]Elizabeth Kilham, "Sketches in Color," *Putnam's Monthly*, 15 (New York: March 1870): 304-311.

[33]Kilham, "Sketches in Color," 304-311.

[34]Holland, ed., *The Letters and Diary of Laura M. Towne*, 22.

[35]Pearson, ed., *Letters from Port Royal, 1862-1868*, 68-69.

[36]Bellah, "Civil Religion in America," 7, 11. Bellah shows how Thanksgiving, Memorial Day, Independence Day, and other national holidays provide an annual ritual calendar for the civil religion; Billington, *The Journal of Charlotte Forten*, 153, 265; Speech first read on Saint Helena Island, 23 November 1862, printed in *The Liberator* (December 26, 1862).

[37]Thomas W. Higginson, *Army Life in a Black Regiment*, (East Lansing: Michigan State University Press, 1960 [1870]): 30. Higginson is the ideal example of the apostle of the American religion. At Harvard he read omnivorously in six languages, and entered Harvard Divinity School following his undergraduate years. A young idealist, he feared the corruptions of professional life but eventually pastored the Free Church in Worcester. He soon turned his skills toward writing about reform. When war broke out, the military recruited Higginson to command the first black regiment, all former slaves in South Carolina who distinguished themselves in combat. See the above volume's introduction by Howard Mumford Jones for further information.

[38]Pearson, ed., *Letters from Port Royal, 1862-1868*, 130; Holland, ed., *The Letters and Diary of Laura M. Towne*, 99.

[39]Billington, ed., *The Journal of Charlotte L. Forten*, 171f.

[40]Grace B. House, "The Fiftieth Anniversary of Penn School," *Southern Workman* (May, 1912): 319; Jacoway, *Yankee Missionaries in the South*, 87; Holland, ed., *Letters and Diary of Laura M. Towne*, 162.

[41]Bellah, "Civil Religion in America," 11.

[42]Towne, *Letters and Diary*, 286, 266, 295f, 304.

[43]Kilham, "Sketches in Color," 123. Late nineteenth-century African-American religious culture will be discussed in more detail in chapter three.

[44]*Freedmen's Journal* (New England Freedmen's Aid Society, January 1, 1865): 3; Susan King Taylor, *Reminiscences of My Life in Camp* (New York: Arno Press, 1968 [1902]): 67.

[45]Rose, *Rehearsal for Reconstruction*; T. Harry Williams "The North Carolina Historical Review," critique listed on backcover of Rose's book.

[46]Holland, ed., *The Letters and Diary of Laura M. Towne*, 135.

[47]"Diary of Laura Towne," vol. 1, Penn School Papers, Southern Historical Collection, University of North Carolina, reel 18; *A Cycle of Letters*, vol. 1, p. 160, Penn School Papers, reel 18. As the war progressed, many Union soldiers embraced the ideals of emancipation.

[48]Holland, ed., *The Letters and Diary of Laura M. Towne*, 60; George Hendricks, "Union Army Occupation of the Southern Seaboard, 1861-1865" (Ph.D dissertation, Georgia Institute of Technology): 26; Pierce, "The Freedmen at Port Royal," 298.

[49]Holland, ed., *The Letters and Diary of Laura M. Towne*, 102-3; see also Pearson, ed., *Letters from Port Royal, 1862-1868*, 51, 155.

[50]Holland, ed., *The Letters and Diary of Laura M. Towne*, 41-42, 44-45, 107.

[51]Holland, ed., *The Letters and Diary of Laura M. Towne*, 100.

[52]Pearson, ed., *Letters from Port Royal, 1862-1868*, 135.

[53]Johnson, *A Social History of the Sea Islands*, 185-86; Holland, ed., *The Letters and Diary of Laura M. Towne*, 101; W. C. Gannet to E. S. Gannett, February 22 [1864]; Pearson, ed., *Letters from Port Royal, 1862-1868*; William Pease, "Three Years Among the Freedmen," 107-112.

[54]"The Sea Islands," *Harper's New Monthly Magazine*, 57 (November, 1878): 855; Holland, ed., *The Letters and Diary of Laura M. Towne*, 101, 106, 129, 139, 174, 176.

[55]David Donald, ed., *Inside Lincoln's Cabinet, The Civil War Diaries of Salmon P. Chase* (New York, 1954): 71; William H. Pease, "William Channing

Gannett" (Ph.D dissertation, University of Rochester, 1955); Tomlinson to McKim, August 18, 1862, McKim Manuscript, Cornell University; Arthur Sumner to Nina Hartshorn, August 8, 1864, Penn School Papers, Southern Historical Collection, University of North Carolina at Chapel Hill.

[56]Rose, *Rehearsal for Reconstruction*, 218.

[57]Rose, *Rehearsal for Reconstruction*, 219; Holland, ed., *The Letters and Diary of Laura M. Towne*, 32, 127, 256.

[58]Drake, "The American Missionary Association"; James M. McPherson, "White Liberals and Black Power in Negro Education, 1865-1915," *American Historical Review*, 75 (June 1970): 1357-58. In 1861, the AMA committed almost all its financial resources to African-American education. Northern evangelical churches joined the effort and these schools supplied almost all the higher education for Southern blacks until the twentieth century. W.E.B. DuBois wrote that it was the "finest thing in American history, and one of the few things untainted by sordid greed and cheap vainglory." See McPherson, 1358.

[59]Botume, *First Days Amongst the Contrabands*, 107-109.

[60]George Stetson, "The Negro's Need in Education," *The Unitarian Review* (February 1887): 137.

[61]John Hunn, *New York Nation*, 14 December 1865; Pearson, ed., *Letters from Port Royal, 1862-1868*, 287.

[62]Lewis S. Gannett to Courtney Siceloff, 20 May 1954, Penn Newsletter, Autumn 1954, Penn School Papers, reel 16.

[63]Obituary of French, *Beaufort Tribune*, 22 March 1876; Rose, *Rehearsal for Reconstruction*, 393-394.

[64]Holland, ed., *The Letters and Diary of Laura M. Towne*, 228, 230, 242; Penn School Papers, reel 1. It should be noted that Martha Schofield, who initially taught on the Sea Islands, moved in 1868 to Aiken, South Carolina, where she served the African-American community for 48 years.

[65]Bellah, "Civil Religion in America," 9-11; Sidney Mead, *The Lively Experiment* (New York, 1963): 12; Penn School Papers, reel 1, February 15, 1873; "Principal's Report by Ellen Murray, 20 June 1903," Penn School Papers, reel 1; Botume, *First Day Amongst the Contrabands*, 88-89, 125.

[66]Bellah, "Civil Religion in America," 9-10; [J. C. French] *The Trip of the Steamer Oceanus to Fort Sumter and Charleston, S.C.* (Brooklyn, 1865): 58-75; Rose, *Rehearsal for Reconstruction*, 343-345.

[67]Holland, ed., *The Letters and Diary of Laura M. Towne*, 310.

Notes to Chapter 3:

[1]Grace Bigelow House, "How Freedom Came to Big Pa," *The Southern Workman*, 45 (April 1916): 220-225.

[2]Edward Pierce to S. P. Chase, Secretary of the Treasury, 2 June 1862, *The Rebellion Record*, supplement vol. 1, ed. Frank Moore (New York: G. P. Putnam, 1864): 316; Jackson, "Educational Efforts of the Freedmen's Bureau," 33; Holland, *The Letters and Diaries of Laura M. Towne*, 270.

[3]Interview with Sara Singleton, born 1917, grand-daughter of Nancy, June 1996 on Saint Helena Island.

[4]Jeanette Robinson Murphy, "The Survival of African Music in America," *Popular Science Monthly* 55 (New York, 1899): 666; Pierce, "The Negroes at Port Royal, SC," 305; Holland, *The Letters and Diaries of Laura M. Towne*, 107, 281.

[5]Holland, *The Letters and Diaries of Laura M. Towne*, 232, 186; Creel, *A Peculiar People*, 274; Raboteau, *Slave Religion*.

[6]Patricia Jones-Jackson, *When Roots Die* (Athens, GA: University of Georgia Press, 1987): 91-92, 77-82

[7]John S. Mbiti, *African Religions and Philosophy* (New York: Doubleday and Co., 1970); Harold Carter, *The Prayer Tradition of Black People* (Valley Forge, PA: Judson Press, 1976); Botume, *First DaysAmongst the Contrabands*, 75.

[8]Pearson, *Letters from Port Royal*, 122, 249; Botume, *First Days Amongst the Contrabands*, 166-167.

[9]Creel, *A Peculiar People*, 263; George P. Rawick, *The American Slave: South Carolina Narratives* II (Westport, CT: Greenwood Publishing, 1972): 180-181.

[10]Thomas W. Higginson, "Negro Spirituals," *Atlantic Monthly* (June 1867): 685-694. Higginson commented on these songs' symbolic, political nature, but he remained convinced that the songs' spiritual character

endured. While certain references to "crossing the river" indicate escape to the North, others clearly refer to life after death. One song stated, "We'll cross de danger water . . . We'll cross de mighty Myo." An old man told Higginson it was the river of death. Higginson reported that the West African word "Mawa" means to die. Turner reports the following translations for similar West African words which appear in Gullah: "maide" - death, "mawu" - God. See Turner, *Africanisms in the Gullah Dialect,* 130; John Mason Brown, "Songs of the Slaves," *Lippincott's Magazine* II (December 1868): 618-619.

[11]Sterling Stuckey, *Slave Culture* (New York: Oxford University Press, 1987): 27; Brown, "Songs of the Slaves," 111; Pearson, *Letters from Port Royal,* 26-27.

[12]Melville J. Herskovits, *Dahomey* (New York: Augustin Press, 1938): 1:216; Melville J. Herskovits, *Rebel Destiny* (New York: Whittlesey House, McGraw-Hill, 1934): 8-9; Stuckey, *Slave Culture,* 11-15; Mary Arnold Twining, "Movement and Dance on the Sea Islands," *Journal of Black Studies,* 15 (June 1985): 467. Frazier, *The Negro Church in America,* 1; Mary Arnold Twining, "An Examination of African Folk Culture of the South Carolina and Georgia Sea Islands," Ph.D. dissertation, Indiana University, 1977; Abigail M. Holmes Christensen, "Spirituals and Shouts of Southern Negroes," *Journal of American Folklore,* 7 (1894): 155; Mary Douglas, *Implicit Meanings* (London: Routledge & Kegan Paul, 1975): 153; Claude Levi-Strauss, "The Structural Study of Myth," *Journal of American Folklore,* 28 (1955): 428-444.

[13]This analogy was used to ask cultural questions in an interview with archaeologist William Dever. See *Biblical Archaeology Review* (September/October 1996): 33.

[14]Pearson, *Letters from Port Royal,* 27; William Gannett and E. E. Hale, "The Freedmen at Port Royal," *North American Review,* 101 (July 1865): 10; Holland, *The Letters and Diaries of Laura M. Towne,* 22; Charlotte Forten, "Life on the Sea Islands," *Atlantic Monthly* (May 1864): 593; T. W. Higginson, "Under the Palmetto," *Continental Monthly,* 4 (1863): 196-197.

[15]Sir Charles Lyell, *Second Visit to the United States* I, (New York, 1849): 269-270; Pearson, *Letters from Port Royal,* 27; Julia Peterkin, *Scarlet Sister Mary* (Dunwoody, GA: Norman S. Berg, Pub., 1928): 17; Clifton H. Johnson, ed., *God Struck Me Dead: Religious Conversion Experiences and Autobiographies of Ex-Slaves* (Philadelphia: Pilgrim Press, 1969): 153.

[16]John S. Mbiti, *Introduction to African Religion* (Portsmouth, NH: Heinemann Educational Books, 1991): 54-61.

[17]While several scholars refer to this phrase "catching sense," I was told by an islander that the phrase was never used by the local people. Reverend Kenneth Doe of Saint Joseph's Baptist Church on Saint Helena believes the phrase to be a creation of folklore writers.

[18]Mbiti, *Introduction to African Religion,* 98-103; Patricia Guthrie, "Catching Sense: The Meaning of Plantation Membership on Saint Helena Island, SC," (Ph.D. dissertation, University of Rochester 1977); David Franklin Thorpe Papers, 25 January 1863, Southern Historical Collection, Wilson Library University of North Carolina, Box 1.

[19]*Southern Christian Advocate,* 18 April 1843; 28 July 1843; 6 September 1859; Charles A. Raymond, "The Religious Life of the Negro Slave," *Harper's New Monthly Magazine* 27 (October 1863): 680; Johnson, ed., *God Struck Me Dead,* 114.

[20]Charles A. Raymond, "The Religious Life of the Negro Slave," *Harper's New Monthly Magazine,* 27 (October 1863): 680; Higginson, "Negro Spirituals," 688; *Southern Christian Advocate,* October 30, 1846, October 30, 1847; Pearson, *Letters from Port Royal,* 43-44; Holland, *The Letters and Diaries of Laura M. Towne,* 144; Gannett and Hale, "The Freedmen at Port Royal," 10.

[21]Lawton, "The Religious Life of South Carolina Coastal and Sea Island Negroes," 138; Higginson, "Negro Spirituals," 688. The Gullah dialect is indifferent to gender in its use of pronouns. Men and women are "he."

[22]Pearson, *Letters from Port Royal,* 28; Botume, *First Days Amongst the Contrabands,* 254-255; *Southern Christian Advocate,* 30 October 1846, 30 October 1847.

[23]Holland, *The Letters and Diaries of Laura M. Towne,* 258.

[24]Holland, *The Letters and Diaries of Laura M. Towne,* 79; Raymond, "The Religious Life of the Negro Slave," 680.

[25]Creel, *A Peculiar People,* 295; David Franklin Thorpe Papers, 25 January 1863; Murphy, "The Survival of African Music in America," 333; Pearson, *Letters from Port Royal,* 145, 249, 268.

[26]Peterkin, *Scarlet Sister Mary,* 17.

[27]Botume, *First Days Amongst the Contrabands,* 104-105, 84-85.

[28]Botume, *First Days Amongst the Contrabands,* 218; Creel, *A Peculiar*

People, 264-266; Billington, *The Journal of Charlotte L. Forten*, 166; Paul Radin, "Status, Fantasy, and the Christian Dogma," *God Struck Me Dead*, ed. Clifton Johnson, ix.

[29]Holland, *The Letters and Diaries of Laura M. Towne*, 42.

[30]George Stetson, "The Negro's Need in Education," *Unitarian Review* (February 1887): 143; Holland, *The Letters and Diaries of Laura M. Towne*, 252.

[31]Howard, "Before and After Emancipation," 142-143.

[32]Arthur Sumner to Nina Hartshorn, 18 May 1862, Penn School Papers, vol. 4, Southern Historical Collection.

[33]Holland, *The Letters and Diaries of Laura M. Towne*, 163; "The South as It Is," *The Nation* (November 30, 1865): 682.

[34]Gannett and Hale, "The Freedmen at Port Royal," 10, Churches practicing "closed communion" only allow their own church members to receive the bread and wine during communion. Non-Christians and even members of other churches are not welcome at the Lord's Supper.

[35]Laura Towne to J. M. McKim, 1 July and 2 August 1862, Penn School Papers, Southern Historical Collection, University of North Carolina, Chapel Hill; Pearson, *Letters from Port Royal*, 145; Holland, *The Letters and Diaries of Laura M. Towne*, 92, 129, 279; Pearson, *Letters from Port Royal*, 145, 269; Gannett and Hale, "The Freedmen at Port Royal," 9; Records at Brick Baptist Church, Saint Helena Island, South Carolina.

[36]Creel, *A Peculiar People*, 295; Pearson, *Letters from Port Royal*, 145.

[37]Stetson, "The Negro's Need in Education," 143; Murphy, "The Survival of African Music in America," 662; Creel, *A Peculiar People*, 182; Thomas Turpin, *Christian Advocate Journal*, 31 January 1834.

[38]Pearson, *Letters from Port Royal*, 287, 286.

[39]Holland, *Letters and Diary of Laura M. Towne*, 162.

[40]Higginson, "Under the Palmetto," 201; Pearson, *Letters from Port Royal*, 166; Mary Ames, *From a New England Woman's Diary in Dixie in 1865* (New York: Negro Universities Press, 1969 [1906]: 31; Carter G. Woodson, *Education of the Negro Prior to 1861* (Arno Press, 1968 [1919]): 221.

[41]Pearson, *Letters from Port Royal*, 65.

[42]Botume, *First Days Amongst the Contrbands*, 254.

[43]Howard, "Before and After Emancipation," 140-141.

[44]Pearson, *Letters from Port Royal*, 15, 25, 125; Kilham, "Sketches in Color," 308.

[45]Margaret Weary as told to Rachel Crane Mather, *Port Royal Under Six Flags* (Bobbs-Merrill, 1960): 319; Jeff Rosenfeld, "The Forgotten Hurricane," *Weatherwise* (Washington: American Meteorological Society, August-September 1993): 13-17.

[46]Rosenfeld, "The Forgotten Hurricane," 18; Gannett and Hale, "The Freedmen at Port Royal," 10-11

Notes to Chapter 4:

[1]Rossa Cooley, *Homes of the Freed* (New Republic, Inc., 1926): 15-23; Elizabeth Jacoway, *Yankee Missionaries in the South*, 57; Frances Eliot Foote, "A Pioneer in the New South," *Boston Evening Transcript*, 12 November 1904, in The Penn School Papers, Southern Historical Collection, University of North Carolina, Chapel Hill.

[2]Rossa Cooley, Easter Sermon 1921, Penn School Papers, reel 2; for examples of social gospel material read, see "Notebook of Grace B. House," books read in 1911, Penn School Papers, reel 26.

[3]Grace House, "The Promise of Better Days," *Southern Workman* (October, 1908): 547-551.

[4]S. C. Armstrong to Laura Towne, 9 November 187? (no later than 1872), Penn School Papers, reel 1; Jacoway, *Yankee Missionaries in the South*, 33; Leo M. Favrot, *Southern Workman*, 46 (October 1917): 572.

[5]Elizabeth Jacoway's work thoroughly covers the Penn board of trustees. In many ways, her work is more a study of the board than a study of Cooley and House.

[6]Rossa Cooley, "Service to Penn School," *Southern Workman* (October 1917): 605; Jacoway, *Yankee Missionaries in the South*, 30-34; January 15, 1901, May 27, 1903, Penn School Papers, reel 1.

[7]Jacoway, *Yankee Missionaries in the South*, 37. One significant demonstration of Dawkins's authority is that the Board's treasurer sent all money directly to Mr. Dawkins rather than to Miss Murray. See Peabody to Jenks, 10 January 1903, Penn School Papers.

[8]Septima Poinsette Clark, *Echo in My Soul* (New York: E. P. Dutton & Co., Inc., 1962): 36. Septima Clark, a Charleston native, taught in South Carolina schools from 1916-1956. In 1956 she became the Director of Education at the Highlander Folk School in Tennessee. In 1961, she began full-time work with the Southern Christian Leadership Conference leading Citizenship Schools on the Sea Islands including the Penn Center on Saint Helena.

[9]Annual Report, 1903 and 1904, Penn School Papers.

[10]Dawkins received glowing reports in several articles including: H. W. Foote, "The Penn School on Saint Helena Island," *Southern Workman* (May 1902): 269; Niels Christensen, "The Negroes of Beaufort County, South Carolina," *Southern Workman* (October 1903): 485; Grace House, "The Penn School and the Farmers' Conference," *Southern Workman* (January 1907): 60; Board of Trustee's Minutes, 20 January 1903, Penn School Papers; Annual Report, 1904, Penn School Papers; Minutes of Trustees, 20 January 1903, Penn School Papers.

[11]Ullin W. Leavell, "Trends of Philanthropy in Negro Education," *Journal of Negro Education* (January 1933): 42; Buttrick to Peabody, 15 June 1903, James McBride Dabbs Papers, Southern Historical Collection, University of North Carolina, Chapel Hill; Robert D. Jenks to Francis R. Cope, Jr., 6 and 8 July 1903, Penn School Papers, reel 1. Murray possessed little influence after 1905, but remained at Penn until she died in 1908.

[12]Cooley, *Homes of the Freed*, 86f; *Poughkeepsie Eagle*, 30 November 1926, Penn School Papers, reel 27, volume 77; Robert D. Jenks to Francis R. Cope, Jr., 6 and 8 July 1903, Penn School Papers, reel 1.

[13]Grace B. House, "Notebook of Grace B. House," December 31, 1899, Penn School Papers, reel 26, vol 66-A. Scripture text found in Phillipians 3:13-14.

[14]House, "Notebook of Grace B. House," December 31, 1902, December 31, 1902, Penn School Papers, reel 26, vol 66-A.

[15]House, "Notebook of Grace B. House," October 30, 1900; January 1, 1901; December 28, 1902; March 1, 1903; December 13, 1903; December 30, 1906, all in Penn School Papers, reel 26, vol 66-A.

[16]Jacoway, *Yankee Missionaries in the South*; T. R. Mitchell and R. Lowe, "To Sow Contentment: Philanthropy, Scientific Agriculture and the Making of the New South: 1906-1920," *Journal of Social History*, 24 (Winter, 1990): 316-335. Jacoway accuses Penn's trustees of various ulterior motives but the board consisted of many shining personalities. Francis Cope, Paul Brown, Harold Evans, John Silver, and William Cadbury were all Quakers devoted to social progress. Paul Kellogg was a social reformer deeply involved in supporting labor, public housing, urban renewal, rights of women workers, and conservation of natural resources. For forty years he served as chief editor over the *Survey*, the leading journal of social work.

[17]Rossa B. Cooley, "Address on Education," November 19, 20, 21, and 22, 1908, Penn School Papers, reel 1.

[18]June 1996 interview with Sara Singleton, resident of Saint Helena Island since 1917; Grace B. House, "The Need and Value of Industrial Education for Negroes," *The Human Way* (Nashville: Southern Sociological Congress, 1913): 89, 95; Rossa Cooley, "Roads to Learning on St. Helena," *Progressive Education*, 14 (April 1937): 247; Cooley, *Homes of the Freed*, 27-30.

[19]Timothy Smith, "Progressivism in American Education," *Harvard Educational Review*, 31 (1961): 176; Lawrence A. Cremin, *The Transformation of the School*, (New York: Alfred A. Knopf, 1961): 128-145, 282-285; L. H. Bailey, *The Nature Study Idea: An Interpretation of the New School Movement to Put the Young into Relation and Sympathy with Nature* (New York: Macmillan Company, 1909).

[20]Thomas Jesse Jones, *Negro Education: A Study of the Private and Higher Schools for Colored People in The United States* (Washington, DC: Department of the Interior, 1917): 483; J. E. Davis, "A Unique People's School," *Southern Workman* (April 1914): 224.

[21]Weatherford, born in 1875, earned a Ph.D. from Vanderbilt and was immediately recruited by Dr. John Mott to work with the YMCA encouraging Southern college students to volunteer their lives to the work of Christ in reforming the world. Like Cooley's "abundant life" message, Weatherford was known as the "prophet of plenty." The writer of over twenty books and a professor at Fisk University, he believed that education could lead people to a better life. In 1962, at the age of 87, he was still busy, attaining national prominence as the initiator and director of research on the groundbreaking book *The Southern Appalachian Region: A Survey*. See Wilma Dykeman, *Prophet of Plenty* (Knoxville: University of Tennessee Press, 1966).

[22]Weatherford to Cooley, 23 February 1915, Penn School Papers, reel 2;

YMCA secretary to Cooley, 27 February 1917, Penn School Papers, reel 2; "1925 Year Book of Penn School," in T. J. Woofter, Jr., *Black Yeomanry* (New York: Henry Holt and Company, 1930): 291.

[23]Walter Rauschenbusch, *The Social Principles of Jesus* (New York: Association Press, 1919).

[24]W. D. Weatherford, "First Steps in Solving the Race Problem," *Southern Workman* (November 1910): 589-590; "Guest Book," Weatherford to Cooley and House, December 1913, Penn School Papers, reel 26.

[25]House, "Notebook of Grace B. House," 31 December 1907, Penn School Papers, reel 26.

[26]Rossa Cooley, "Is There an Explanation?," *The Survey* (13 September 1919): 858; W. D. Weatherford, *Present Forces in Negro Education* (New York: Association Press, 1912): 35; W. D. Weatherford, *Negro Life in the South* (New York: Association Press, 1911): 156; Weatherford, "First Steps in Solving the Race Problem," 591; Rossa Cooley, "Education in the Soil," *Progressive Education* (December 1933): 455; W. D. Weatherford, "The Basis of Understanding Between the Races," *Southern Workman* (1916): 655-659.

[27]"Guest Book, 1905-1962," October 1924; December 1925, Penn School Papers, reel 26, vol 66-B.

[28]"Guest Book, 1905-1962," February 1927; October 1927; April 1930, all in Penn School Papers, reel 26, vol 66-B; 10 May 1926, Mabel Carney to House, Penn School Papers, reel 4.

[29]Jacoway, *Yankee Missionaries in the South*, 116; "The Aims of Penn School," 1926, Penn School Papers; Charles W. Dabney, "Penn School, St. Helena Island," *Southern Workman* (June 1931): 280; Rossa Cooley, "The Negro in His Own Environment," *Vassar Quarterly* (May 1920): 181.

[30]House to Cooley, 21 September 1925 Trustees Meeting, Penn School Papers.

Notes to Chapter 5:

[1]Weatherford, *Negro Life in the South*, 119; W.T.B. Williams, "The Yankee Schoolma'am in Negro Education," *Southern Workman* (February 1915): 77.

[2]Jones, *Negro Education*, 481; Cooley, "Education in the Soil," 454; E.

Durkheim, *The Elementary Forms of the Religious Life* (London: Allen and Unwin, 1915); Douglas, *Implicit Meanings*,142-149; Victor Turner, *The Forest of Symbols* (New York: Cornell University Press, 1967); Victor Turner, *The Drums of Affliction* (Oxford: Claredon Press, 1968).

[3]Dabney, "Penn School, St. Helena Island," 280-281; the phrase is found in the Gospel of John 10:10 in the New Testament.

[4]Rossa Cooley, *School Acres*, (New Haven, CT: Yale University Press, 1930): 26; Cooley, "The Negro in His Own Environment," 181.

[5]Rossa Cooley's Syllabus for Bible Course 1897, Penn School Papers, reel 19, vol. 7, pages 1, 2, 7, 30, 82, 97; Williams, "The Yankee Schoolma'am in Negro Education," 77.

[6]House, "Notebook of Grace B. House," 6 October 1901, 9 August 1903, Penn School Papers, reel 26; Guest Book 1905-1962, March 1923, Penn School Papers, reel 26, vol. 65-B; "The Aims of Penn School," 1926, Penn School Papers. House's notebooks have been rarely utilized by scholars seeking to understand the Penn mission. More than any other Penn personality, Grace House left an extensive record of her inner life and motivations.

[7]Lawton, "The Religious Life of South Carolina Coastal and Sea Island Negroes," 237; Cooley, *School Acres*, 135-136.

[8]Lawton, "The Religious Life of South Carolina Coastal and Sea Island Negroes," 238; Cooley, *School Acres*, 136.

[9]Cooley, *School Acres*, 136.

[10]Guthrie, "Catching Sense; Cooley, *School Acres*, 152; Stephen D. Glazier, "Mourning in the Afro-Baptist Traditions," *The Southern Quarterly*, 23 (Spring 1985): 141-146; Stephen Glazier, *Marchin' the Pilgrims Home: Leadership and Decision-Making in an Afro-Caribbean Faith* (Westport, CT: Greenwood, 1983): 54-58. According to Glazier, congregations of the "Spiritual Baptist" function on Trinidad, St. Vincent, Grenada, Guyana, and New York City.

[11]Cooley, *School Acres*, 150-152; Lawton, "The Religious Life of South Carolina Coastal and Sea Island Negroes," 143. The origins of the "seeking ritual" have been discussed above in chapters 1 and 3.

[12]Elsie Clews Parsons, *Folk-Lore of the Sea Islands, South Carolina* (New York: American Folk-Lore Society, 1923): 204; Lawton, "The Religious Life of

South Carolina Coastal and Sea Island Negroes," 144. In the 1930s, Lawton recorded numerous conversations describing religious visions.

[13]Robert Simpson, "The Shout and Shouting in Slave Religion of the United States," *The Southernly Quarterly*, 23 (Spring 1985): 43-45; Raymond, "The Religious Life of the Negro Slave," 819-820; Barbara Myerhoff, "Rites of Passage," *Celebration: Studies in Festivity and Ritual*, ed. Victor Turner (Washington, DC: Smithsonian Institution Press, 1982): 111-115.

[14]Lawton, "The Religious Life of South Carolina Coastal and Sea Island Negroes," 140-149; Interview with Rebecca Middleton on St. Helena, June 1996; Parsons, *Folk-Lore of the Sea Islands*, 204.

[15]Mechal Sobel, *Trabelin' On: The Slave Journey to an Afro-Baptist Faith* (Westport, CT: Greenwood, 1979); Lawton, "The Religious Life of South Carolina Coastal and Sea Island Negroes," 148-149, 153, 156; author unknown, "Folklore and Ethnology," *Southern Workman*, 24 (September 1895): 279. My own grandmother told my father that dreams concerning muddy water signified death.

[16]Glazier, *Marchin' the Pilgrims Home*, 150, 155; Sigmund Freud, *The Basic Writings of Sigmund Freud*, ed. A. A. Brill (New York: Random House, 1938): 183, 192, 208, 215. My intention here is not to "psychologize" faith and ritual. Analysis of these dreams and visions is not meant to be reductionistic. Psychoanalytic theory can shed light on these phenomena without fully explaining them.

[17]Johnson, *God Struck Me Dead*, 140.

[18]James Hillman, *A Blue Fire: Selected Writings by James Hillman*, ed. Thomas Moore (New York: Harper and Row, 1989).

[19]P. Smiley, ed., *Folklore from Virginia, South Carolina, Georgia, Alabama and Florida* (American Folklore Society, 1919): 240; Newbell Puckett, *Folk Beliefs of Southern Negroes* (Chapel Hill: University of North Carolina Press, 1926): 542.

[20]Lawton, "The Religious Life of South Carolina Coastal and Sea Island Negroes," 150-155.

[21]Recorded December 29, 1934 by Lawton, "The Religious Life of South Carolina Coastal and Sea Island Negroes," 161.

[22]Johnson, *God Struck Me Dead*, 13, 91.

[23]Lawton, "The Religious Life of South Carolina Coastal and Sea Island Negroes," 142.

[24]Interview with Sara Singleton on Saint Helena, June 1996. Many of the symbols mentioned here were common to the local lore. A baby represented the soul, the little person who lives inside. The travel gown, tickets, and letter were common visions. See Lawton, "The Religious Life of South Carolina Coastal and Sea Island Negroes," 150-153.

[25]Jones, *Negro Education*, 84; Cooley, *School Acres*, 81; Sermon in Chapel, November 21, 1921, Penn School Papers, reel 2; Smith, "Progressivism in American Education"; Unknown author, "The Real Aim of Industrial Schools," *Southern Workman* (January 1908): 374-375. The *Southern Workman*, the journal of the industrial education movement, featured articles concerning the Penn School almost every year from 1900 until 1936.

[26]Cooley, *School Acres*, 81; Cooley, "Education in the Soil," 454.

[27]Mitchell and Lowe, "To Sow Contentment," 319; Weatherford, *Present Forces in Negro Education*, 35; Commonplace Book of Grace B. House, June 1908; 17 July 1908, Penn School Papers, reel 26, vol. 66-B.

[28]"Historical Handbook of Penn School and Saint Helena Island, South Carolina," (not published), Howard Kester Papers, Southern Historical Collection, University of North Carolina at Chapel Hill; Cooley, "Education in the Soil," 455.

[29]Cooley, *School Acres*, 27-29. This building project started a 90-year tradition which continues today on the island. Penn still hosts camps that repair homes on the Sea Islands.

[30]Cooley, *School Acres*, 28; John Dewey, *The School and Society* (Chicago, 1899): 23-24; Cremin, *Transformation of the School*, 118.

[31]House, "The Need and Value of Industrial Education for Negroes," 89; Cooley, "Roads to Learning on St. Helena," 247; Cooley, "Education in the Soil," 453; Cooley, *School Acres*, 99-101; Cooley to Contributors, 8 May 1930, Penn School Papers.

[32]W. D. Weatherford, "Negro Training in the South," *Southern Workman* (October 1912):556; Cooley, *Homes of the Freed*, 165.

[33]Cooley, *School Acres*, 46; Charles Kraft, *Christianity with Power* (Ann

Arbor, MI: Vine Books, 1989): 4; Cooley, "The Negro in His Own Environment," 181.

[34]Bellah, "Civil Religion in America," 2; Grace B. House, "The Penn School and the Farmer's Conference," *Southern Workman* (January 1907): 58-60; Cooley, *School Acres*, 117.

[35]Seaman Knapp, "The Mission of Cooperative Demonstration Work in the South," U.S. Department of Agriculture, Circular of Information 33 (Washington, DC: 1910): 7; Mitchell and Lowe, "To Sow Contentment," 318.

[36]Cooley, *School Acres*, 109-111; House, "The Penn School and the Farmer's Conference," 58; House, "The Need and Value of Industrial Education," 97.

[37]Salter, "Changing Economic Patterns of the South Carolina Sea Islands," 163; Clark, *Echo in My Soul*, 42. In contrast to these early efforts in 1912, most of coastal Carolina did not form cooperatives until the late 1930s. Septima Clark wrote that a lack of cooperative societies on other islands had contributed to extremely crude living conditions.

[38]Bascom, "Acculturation Among the Gullah Negroes," 44; Little, "The Role of the Secret Society in Cultural Specialization," 199-207; Elaine Nichols, *The Last Miles of the Way: African American Homegoing Traditions* (Columbia, SC: Dependable Printing Company, Inc., 1989): 23-25; Howard, "Before and After Emancipation," 142-143.

[39]Cooley, *School Acres*, 115; Dabbs, *Sea Island Diary*, 221-222; Francis Harold Jordon, "Across the Bridge," unpublished Ed.D. dissertation, University of South Carolina, 1991; Record of Pastors at Brick Baptist Church, Saint Helena Island.

[40]October 1911, Penn School Papers, reel 1; J. E. Davis, "A Unique People's School," *Southern Workman* (April 1914): 226; Cooley, *School Acres*, 119.

[41]Cooley, *School Acres*, 120-121. These cooperative efforts often did not occur on those sea islands outside the influence of Penn. Even today, on several islands the lack of ditching has contributed to a variety of problems.

[42]House, "The Need and Value of Industrial Education for Negroes," 95; Cooley's Message in Chapel, November 11, 1921, Penn School Papers, reel 2.

[43]Cooley, *School Acres*, 112-113; Cooley, "Roads of Learning on Saint Helena," 250.

[44]June 1996 interview with Kathryn Austen, life-time resident of Saint Helena, who attended Penn School, and presently is employed at Penn Center. "Miss Cooley made me do chores on school farm if I mis-behaved, and I did like to mis-behave. Miss Cooley was strict on discipline. I dearly loved Cooley and House."

Notes to Chapter 6:

[1]Notebook of Grace B. House, [c. 1938], Penn School Papers, reel 26, vol. 66-C; Cooley, *School Acres*, 148, 156; Jacoway, *Yankee Missionaries in the South*, 103.

[2]June 1996 interviews with Kathryn Austen, resident of island; Jacoway, *Yankee Missionaries in the South*, 108; "Two Women on an Atlantic Island," 1932, Penn School Papers; "Annual Report," 1909, 1910, 1917, Penn School Papers.

[3]George Rowe, "The Negroes of the Sea Islands," *Southern Workman* (December 1900): 713; George Kuyper, "The Powerful Influence of a Notable School," *Southern Workman* (January 1931): 30-31; June T. Watkins, "Strategies of Social Control in an Isolated Community: The Case of the Gullah of South Carolina's Saint Helena Island," unpublished Ph.D. dissertation, Indiana University of Pennsylvania, 1993: 120.

[4]Saint Paul's command in 1 Corinthians states, "When any of you has a grievance against another, do you dare to take it to court...Can it be that there is no one among you wise enough to decide between one believer and another?"

[5]Cooley, *School Acres*, 120, 157.

[6]Cooley, *Homes of the Freed*, 52-56; Cooley, *School Acres*, 121.

[7]Lawton, "The Religious Life of South Carolina Coastal and Sea Island Negroes," 146-147.

[8]May 1996 interview with United Methodist minister Charles White, an African American who spent his childhood on the Sea Islands; Lawton, "The Religious Life of South Carolina Coastal and Sea Island Negroes," 140, 167-170.

[9]Christensen, "The Negroes of Beaufort County, South Carolina," 484; Woofter, *Black Yeomanry*, 235-236.

[10]Interview with Rev. Ervine Greene, pastor of Brick Baptist Church, June 1996.

[11]Lawton, "The Religious Life of South Carolina Coastal and Sea Island Negroes," 171; Interviews with Emory Campbell at Penn, December 1994 and June 1996.

[12]Lawton, "The Religious Life of South Carolina Coastal and Sea Island Negroes," 168.

[13]"Still Tongue Make a Wise Head," *South Carolina Humanities Council Speaker's Bureau* (Columbia, SC): 3; Telephone interview with Veronica Davis Gerald, Coastal Carolina University, January 1996; Bascom, "Acculturation Among the Gullah Negroes," 48.

[14]Lawton, "The Religious Life of South Carolina Coastal and Sea Island Negroes," 15, 70-75. In March 1996, I attended a service at Saint Joseph's Baptist Church on the island which was led by a female "prophet." The church responded with great enthusiasm.

[15]House, "The Penn School and the Farmers' Conference," *Southern Workman* (January 1907): 59.

[16]Jacoway, *Yankee Missionaries in the South*, 72-73, 81; Cooley, *Homes of the Freed*; Cooley, *School Acres*, 93-95.

[17]Cooley, *Homes of the Freed*, xiii; Jacoway, *Yankee Missionaries in the South*, 151-152; Cooley, *School Acres*, 97-98; Woofter, *Black Yeomanry*, 106, 111.

[18]Jones, *Negro Education*, 483.

[19]Cooley, "Education in the Soil," 454; Cooley, *School Acres*, 98; 5 February 1914, *Beaufort Gazette*. Discussions for a bridge began in 1913. Elections held in 1914 concerning a bridge showed strong opposition from both Ladies and Saint Helena islands. However, most mainlanders wanted the bridge.

[20]Prayer of Aunt Jane, resident of Saint Helena, recorded by Cooley, *School Acres*, 157-158

Notes to Chapter 7:

[1]Francis Cope's copy of Reid Report, February 1948, Penn School Papers, Southern Historical Collection, University of North Carolina; Cooley to Cadbury, February 2, 1948, Penn School Papers.

[2]Williams, "The Yankee Schoolma'am in Negro Education," 75; W.E.B. DuBois, *From Servitude to Service* (Boston: American Unitarian Association, 1905): 181; W.E.B. DuBois, *The Souls of Black Folk* (New York, 1903): 100.

[3]Jones, *Negro Education*, 483-485; Woofter, *Black Yeomanry*,187, 200; Loram to Cooley, October 6, 1933, March 29, 1934, Penn School Papers.

[4]Assistant Treasurer's Report by Ellen Murray, December 1901, Penn School Papers, reel 1; February 1, 1907, Penn School Papers, reel 1; Expenses Report, June 30, 1911, Penn School Papers, reel 1.

[5]Cooley's Report to Board, January 14, 1913, Penn School Papers, reel 1; Annual Audits, Penn School Papers, reel 23. Between 1913 and 1920, Penn's General Investments rose from $50,440 to $95,840. Much of this was due to the Laura M. Towne fund, donated in 1914, worth $25,878.

[6]Letter to G. C. Mann, December 27, 1921, Penn School Papers, reel 2; Cope to Howell, November 3, 1922, Penn School Papers, reel 2; Peabody to Wood, September 11, 1926, Penn School Papers; Board of Trustees Meeting, October 22, 1926, Penn School Papers; Jacoway, *Yankee Missionaries in the South*, 166-167.

[7]Board of Trustees Meeting, September 20, 1922, Penn School Papers, reel 2; Cooley to Buttrick, December 14, 1922, Penn School papers, reel 2.

[8]Cooley, "Education in the Soil," 454.

[9]Board of Trustee Meeting, July 6, 1942, Penn School Papers, reel 19; Annual Audits, Penn School Papers, reel 23.

[10]Annual Audit, Penn School Papers, reel 23. E. Jacoway describes in extreme detail the financial problems at Penn. In fact, this is a major topic in her book. However, she ignores the large endowment funds, thus painting an extremely poor picture of the financial situation. Jacoway inaccurately states that although the Trustees worked to raise funds, "the endowment fund never materialized." In her final chapter, she seems to imply that Penn was broke when the Kesters arrived, and in reality, nothing could be farther from the truth. See Jacoway, *Yankee Missionaries in the South*, 179.

[11]J. Howard Melish, "George Foster Peabody," *Religion in Life* (Winter 1938): 92; See Wood to Brown, 28 October 1949, Penn School Papers, reel 16.

[12]"The New Because of the Old," *Southern Workman* (March 1929): 111-112; Jacoway, *Yankee Missionaries in the South*, 191-192.

[13]August Meier, *Negro Thought in America* (Ann Arbor, MI: University of Michigan Press, 1963): 227-259; W.E.B. Du Bois, "The Browsing Reader," *Crisis*, 38 (November 1930): 378.

[14]McPherson, "Whites Liberals and Black Power in Negro Education," 1357-1363; Jones, *Negro Education*, 481-483; Interview with Courtney Siceloff, 14 May 1996, Atlanta GA.

[15]Lewis McMillan, "Negro Higher Education as I Have Known It," *Journal of Negro Education* (January 1939): 1-12; Franklin Frazier, *Black Bourgeoisie* (New York: Collier Books, 1962): 56-57; James M. McPherson, *The Abolitionist Legacy* (Princeton, NJ: Princeton University Press, 1976): 199.

[16]Kelly Miller, "The Higher Education of the Negro is at the Crossroads," *Educational Review*, 82 (1926): 273-275; Board of Trustees Meeting, May 26, 1943, Penn School Papers; Cope to Brown, August 17, 1943, Penn School Papers.

[17]McPherson, *The Abolitionist Legacy*, 199; Cremin, *The Transformation of the School*, 181, 349-350.

[18]Trustees' Meeting, 29 February 1944, Penn School Papers, reel 19; Trustees' Meeting, 11 June 1946, Penn School Papers, reel 20. Dr. Harry Richardson, associated with the General Education Board, the Phelps-Stokes Fund, and the Home Mission Council, visited Penn and approved funding of the seminary plan.

[19]Reid Report 1948, Penn School Papers, reel 20; Ira Reid, Evaluation of Penn School, November 1947, Penn School Papers; Cadbury to Penn School Contributors, May 1, 1948, Penn School Papers; Ira Reid to Wood, April 6, 1948, Penn School Papers.

Notes to Chapter 8:

[1]The chapter's title is taken from an article written by Penn's assistant principle. See Grace House, "The Little Foe of All the World," *Southern Workman*, 35 (November 1906): 598-614.

[2]Courtney Siceloff to Tom Jenks, 14 June 1960, Penn School Papers, Southern Historical Collection, University of North Carolina at Chapel Hill, reel 16; Elizabeth Siceloff to Julia Abramson, 17 April 1962, Penn School Papers, reel 16; Dr. George Aull to Courtney Siceloff, 25 June 1959, Penn School papers, reel 16; Jordon, "Across the Bridge," 155-159.

[3]Many older board members resigned in the early 1950s. They were tired of the fund raising and one woman stated that Penn's time was over and she felt unsure if "there is anything to work for." See Grace Smith to Wood, 29 December 1949, Penn School Papers, reel 16; Cadbury to Wood, 2 February 1951, Penn School Papers, reel 16.

[4]Interview with Courtney Siceloff, 14 May 1996, Atlanta, Georgia; Penn Board Meeting, 25 January 1950, Penn School Papers, reel 16.

[5]Penn Board Meeting, 25 January 1950, Penn School Papers, reel 16. Additional information concerning George Mitchell and the Southern Regional Council will be provided below.

[6]J. Isaac Copeland, "Life of Marion Wright," unpublished paper, Carolinian Manuscript Archives, University of South Carolina.

[7]Daniel W. Hollis, *The University of South Carolina* vol 2 (Columbia: USC Press, 1956): 242-259; Samuel Mitchell, "My Neighbor, The Negro," *Southern Workman* (March 1911): 134-142. Mitchell corresponded with the Penn School from 1912 to 1913. See "Guide to the Microfilm Edition of the Penn School Papers," (Chapel Hill: University of North Carolina Library, 1977): 31; Jacoway, *Yankee Missionaries in the South*, 86-87.

[8]Copeland, "Life of Marion Wright"; Dr. Guy Johnson *Folk Culture on Saint Helena Island* (Chapel Hill: University of North Carolina Press, 1930); Anthony Newberry, "Southern Regional Council," *Encyclopedia of Southern Culture*, ed. Charles Wilson and William Ferris (Chapel Hill: University of North Carolina Press, 1989): 1425; Marion Wright, James Dabbs, Alice Spearman, Will Campbell, J. Curtis Dixon, Benjamin Mayes, and George Aull became the Southern members of the Penn board who also served with the Southern Regional Council.

[9]George Mitchell to Elizabeth Siceloff, 27 December 1950, Penn School Papers, reel 16; Mitchell, "My Neighbor, The Negro," 134; James M. Dabbs, *The Road Home* (Philadelphia: Christian Education Press, 1960): 58. The "Student Volunteer Movement" was an amalgam of evangelical and social gospel Christianity. Naturally, this is the same Weatherford connected to Penn in the early 1900s.

[10]James Dabbs, "Toward Christianity," *Churchman* (15 September 1935); James Dabbs "Beyond Tragedy," *Christendom* (Spring 1936).

[11]Jack L. Cooksey, "James McBride Dabbs," *The Item* (Sumter, SC: newspaper; 31 March 1996): 1C; James M. Dabbs, *Haunted By God* (Richmond:

John Knox Press, 1972); Dabbs, *Sea Island Diary*.

[12]Sandra Brenneman Oldendorf, "Highlander Folk School and the South Carolina Sea Island Citizenship Schools" (Ed. D. dissertation, University of Kentucky, 1987): 46-48; Clark, *Echo in My Soul*, 123-132; Cynthia Stokes Brown, ed., *Ready from Within* (Navarro, CA: Wild Trees Press, 1986): 13-19.

[13]David J. Garrow, *Bearing the Cross: Martin Luther King, Jr. and the Southern Christian Leadership Conference* (New York: Vintage Books, 1988): 565; Clark, *Echo in My Soul*, 17, 23, 36, 59, 111.

[14]Clark, *Echo in My Soul*, 113, 118, 119, 157f, 206-213; Aldon Morris, *The Origins of the Civil Rights Movement* (New York: Free Press, 1984): 149.

[15]Dabbs, *Haunted By God*, 133, 138, 147, 160, 178, 188; Dabbs, "Beyond Tragedy."

[16]Clark, *Echo in My Soul*, 132.

[17]Interview with Courtney Siceloff, 14 May 1996, Atlanta. Siceloff was not entirely separated from the Quakers who did hold work camps at Penn beginning in 1952 and hosted annual retreats at Penn during the late 1950s. See 29 October 1957, Report of Director, Penn School Papers, reel 16. Since leaving Penn in 1969, Courtney and Elizabeth Siceloff have been deeply influenced by a yearly conference on "Quaker Life and Doctrine," and by John Puschin, a Quaker theologian emphasizing the cross of Christ and its meaning for today. A Quaker Bible Conference in Honduras has also inspired new ideas about spirituality and community life. Presently living in Atlanta, the Siceloffs operate a weekly Bible study in their home for seekers.

[18]Penn Board Meeting, 12 December 1950, Penn School Papers, reel 16; Memorandum, 11 April 1952, Penn School Papers, reel 16.

[19]Courtney and Elizabeth Siceloff, "A New Birth of Freedom on Saint Helena Island," 1950, Penn School Papers, reel 16.

[20]Interview with Courtney Siceloff; Jordan, "Across the Bridge," 165; Report to Trustees, 9 April 1960, Penn School Papers, reel 16.

[21]Courney and Elizabeth Siceloff, "A New Birth of Freedom on Saint Helena"; Penn Board Meeting, 22 September 1952, Penn School Papers, reel 16; Interview with Courtney Siceloff; Penn Community Services Annual Report 1951, Penn School papers, reel 16.

[22]Pierce, "The Negroes at Port Royal, S.C.," 312.

[23]Courtney Siceloff to Board, 27 November 1950, Penn School Papers, reel 16; Penn Rural Study Team Report, 1960, Penn Community Center Archives, Saint Helena Island; Jordan, "Across the Bridge," 162-163.

[24]Penn News Letter, May 1954, Penn School Papers, reel 16. Interestingly, six students, more than any other group, came from the conservative Citadel Military Institute.

[25]Penn News Letter, May 1954, Penn School Papers, reel 16; Trustees Minutes, 19 November 1956, Penn School Papers, reel 16; Trustees Meeting, 29 October 1957, Penn School Papers, reel 16; Marion Wright to supporters, 25 March 1957, Penn School Papers, reel 16.

[26]Courtney Siceloff to Board Memebers, 5 December 1957, Penn School Papers, reel 16. Siceloff received this letter from Koinonia right after the YMCA canceled the retreat. Out of the Koinonia Farms emerged the organization Habitat for Humanity.

[27]Interview with Courtney Siceloff.

[28]Interview with Courtney Siceloff; Dabbs, "Christian Response to Racial Revolution," 97. Dabbs delivered this sermon on 21 April 1964 at the Acworth Presbyterian Church in Acworth, Georgia.

[29]Oldendorf, "Highlander Folk School," 94-98; G. Carawan and C. Carawan, *Ain't You Got a Right to the Tree of Life* (New York: Simon and Schuster, 1966): 152; Morris, *The Origins of the Civil Rights Movement*, 149-157.

[30]Oldendorf, "Highlander Folk School," 79, 94-98.

[31]Interview with Courtney Siceloff; Telephone interview with Joe McDomick, Penn Center Staff Member, 12 August 1996; Interview with Rev. Kenneth Doe of Saint Joseph's Baptist Church on Saint Helena Island, May 1995; John P. Smith, "Cultural Preservation of the Sea Islands: A Black Social Movement in the Post-Civil Rights Era," *Rural Sociology*, 56 (1991): 288-289.

[32]Consultation on Human Relations, 13-15 May 1960, Penn School Papers, reel 16. Morris College and Benedict College in South Carolina first hosted these schools for black ministers.

[33]Oldendorf, "Highlander Folk School," 42; Garrow, *Bearing the Cross*, 149-151; J. Tracy Powers, *I Will Not Be Silent and I Will Be Heard: Martin*

Luther King, Jr., and the Southern Christian Leadership Conference, and the Penn Center, 1964-1967 (Columbia, SC: South Carolina Department of Archives and History, 1993): 6.

[34]Siceloff to Board, 30 September 1959, Penn School Papers, reel 16; Siceloff to Board, 25 January 1960, Penn School Papers, reel 16; Powers, *I Will Not Be Silent*, 6; Hugh Gibson, "Radical Meetings Shrouded in Secrecy," *Charleston News and Courier*, 13 March 1964; Hugh Gibson, "Dateline Columbia: Frogmore Agenda Presages Trouble," *Charleston News and Courier*, 15 March 1964.

[35]David Garrow, "Where Martin Luther King, Jr. Was Going," *Georgia Historical Quarterly* (Winter 1991): 722-726; Powers, *I Will Not Be Silent*, 12.

[36]Garrow, *Bearing the Cross*, 309.

[37]Newberry, "Southern Regional Council," 1426;

[38]Garrow, *Bearing the Cross*, 282-284; Morris, *The Origins of the Civil Rights Movement*, xiii, 215-226; Board Minutes, 22 April 1964, Penn Community Center Papers, Saint Helena, South Carolina; Siceloff to SNCC, 29 April 1965, Penn Community Center Papers, Saint Helena, South Carolina; Jordon, "Across the Bridge," 159; Interview with Courtney Siceloff.

[39]Powers, *I Will Not Be Silent*, 12-15, 18-22.

[40]Dabbs, "Christian Response to Racial Revolution," 93-94.

[41]Interview with Courtney Siceloff; Jordon, "Across the Bridge," 168.

[42]Jordon, "Across the Bridge," 161; Homer Bigart, "Hunger in America," *New York Times*, 16 February 1969.

Notes to Chapter 9:

[1]Courtney Siceloff to Board, 27 November 1950, Penn School Papers, reel 16.

[2]Alice Wine, interviewed in *Ain't You Got a Right to the Tree of Life*, ed. Carawan and Carawan, 122; Jones-Jackson, *When Roots Die*. Both of these books discuss the unethical means by which the Sea Islands were seized by developers.

[3]William Saunders, interviewed in *Ain't You Got a Right to the Tree of Life*, ed. Carawan and Carawan, 89; Jonathan Green, *Gullah Images: The Art of*

Jonathan Green (Columbia: University of South Carolina Press, 1996): 73; Interview with Emory Campbell, Director of the Penn Center since 1980, *Family Across the Sea*, South Carolina Educational Television Production.

[4]Smith, "Cultural Preservation of the Sea Island Gullah," 285-286; Edward M. Hassinger, *The Rural Component of Society* (Danville, IL: Interstate Press, 1987).

[5]Carroll Greene, Jr., "Coming Home Again," *American Visions* (February 1990): 44-52.

[6]Greene, "Coming Home Again," 47, 50-52; Green, *Gullah Images*, 35-40, 60, 68, 70, 71, 69, 114; Conversation with Rev. Thomas J. Bowman, Saint Mark United Methodist Church in Taylors, South Carolina, concerning African-American funeral practices.

[7]Greene Jr., "Coming Home Again," 44-52.

[8]Johnson, "Across the Bridge," 176.

[9]Karl Mathiason III to Penn Board of Directors, Penn Community Service Papers, Penn Center, Saint Helena Island.

[10]The Peace Corp used Penn as a training base beginning in the mid-1960s. See chapter seven.

[11]Penn Center Heritage Days Celebration Brochure, 10-12 November 1994, Penn Center Archives.

[12]Smith, "Cultural Preservation of the Sea Island Gullah."

[13]Smith, "Cultural Preservation of the Sea Island Gullah," 296; Rev. Ervine Green speaking to the United Methodist Salkshatchie Summer Mission program at Brick Baptist Church, June 1996; Interview with Ervine Green, June 1996.

[14]Kenneth Doe, "The Praise House Tradition and Community Renewal at Saint Joseph Baptist Church," unpublished D.Min. thesis, Erskine Theological Seminary, 1991: 55-60; Interview with Kenneth Doe, May 1995; Attendance at Saint Joseph Baptist Church worship service, March 1996.

[15]Emory Campbell speaking, "Hilton Head Island: A Television History," The Museum on Hilton Head Island, South Carolina.

[16]Rev. Ervine Green speaking to the United Methodist Salkshatchie Summer Mission program at Brick Baptist Church, June 1996; Interview with Ervine Green, June 1996.

[17]Penn Center Heritage Days Celebration Brochure, 10-12 November 1994, Penn Center Archives.

[18]Emory Campbell speaking at the United Methodist Salkehatchie Summer Mission Program at the Penn Center, June 1996; Conversation with Ms. Chris Pendleton, the director of the Museum at Hilton Head Island, September 1996.

[19]Emory Campbell interviewed for the film *Family Across the Sea*, South Carolina Educational Television Production, 1990.

[20]See chapters one and two for discussion of Bunce Island.

[21]*Family Across the Sea*, South Carolina Educational Television Production, 1990.

[22]*Penn Center: A History of Pride, A Future of Promise*, brochure produced by Penn Center in 1990.

[23]DuBois, *From Servitude to Service*, 181.

Bibliography

Personal Interviews

Emory Campbell concerning the Penn Center. Mr. Campbell is the current director of the Penn Center on St. Helena Island.

Courtney Siceloff, director of the Penn Center from 1950 to 1969.

Dr. Kenneth C. Doe, pastor of St. Joseph's Baptist Church on St. Helena Island.

Rev. Ervine Green, pastor of Brick Baptist Church on Saint Helena.

Michael Trinkley concerning archaeological work on the Sea Islands. Dr. Trinkley is President of Chicora Foundation, a public non-profit archaeological organization in South Carolina.

Stanley South on archaeology work. Dr. South works with the South Carolina Institute of Anthropology and Archaeology.

Primary Resources

Christian Advocate and Journal, Wofford College, Spartanburg, South Carolina.

Dabbs, Edith, Papers, Southern Historical Collection, University of North Carolina, Chapel Hill.

Dabbs, James McBride, Papers, Southern Historical Collection, University of North Carolina, Chapel Hill.

Johnson, Guy B., Papers, Southern Historical Collection, University of North Carolina, Chapel Hill.

Kester, Howard, Papers (Microfilm), University of Virgina, Charlottesville.

Penn School Papers, Southern Historical Collection, University of North Carolina, Chapel Hill.

Schofield, Martha, Papers, Southern Historical Collection, University of North Carolina, Chapel Hill.

South Carolina Conference, Methodist Church Archives, Wofford College, Spartanburg, South Carolina.

Southern Christian Advocate, Wofford College, Spartanburg, South Carolina.

Thorpe, David F., Papers, Southern Historical Collection, University of North Carolina, Chapel Hill.

Articles

Benjamin, S. G. "The Sea Islands." *Harper's New Monthly Magazine* 57 (November 1878): 839-861.

Brown, John Mason. "Songs of the Slave." *Lippincott's Magazine* 2 (December 1868): 617-623.

Christensen, Abigail M. Holmes. "Spirituals and Shouts of Southern Negroes." *The Journal of American Folklore* 7 (1894): 154-155.

Christensen, Niels, Jr. "The Negroes of Beaufort County, South Carolina." *Southern Workman* 32 (October 1903): 481-485.

———. "Fifty Years of Freedom: Conditions in the Sea Coast Regions." *Annals of the American Academy of Political and Social Science* 49 (September 1913): 58-66.

Cooley, Rossa B. "Service to Penn School." *Southern Workman* 46 (October 1917): 605-606.

———. "America's Sea Islands." *The Outlook* (30 April 1919): 739-741.

———. "Is There an Explanation?" *The Survey* (13 September 1919): 858.

———. "The Negro in His Own Environment." *Vassar Quarterly* (May 1920): 177-182.

———. "Education in the Soil." *Progressive Education* 8 (December 1933): 448-455.

———. "Tribute to a Faithful Nurse." *Southern Workman* 64 (March 1935): 70-71.

Cope, Francis R. "Service to Penn School." *Southern Workman* 46 (October 1917): 603-605.

Crum, Mason. "The Good Samaritan of St. Helena Island." *South Atlantic Quarterly* 34 (April 1935): 145-149.

C.W.D. "Contraband Singing" *Dwight's Journal of Music* 19 (7 September, 1861): 182.

Dabney, Charles William. "Penn School, St. Helena Island." *Southern Workman* 60 (June 1931): 277-281.

Davis, J. E. "A Unique People's School." *Southern Workman* 43 (April 1914): 217-228.

Editors of *Southern Workman*. "Folklore and Ethnology." *Southern Workman* 24 (September 1895): 154-156.

"Ellen Murray." *Southern Workman* 37 (February 1908): 71-73.

Foote, Henry Wilder. "The Penn School on St. Helena Island." *Southern Workman* 31 (May 1902): 263-270.

Forten, Charlotte. "Life on the Sea Islands." *Atlantic Monthly* (May 1864): 587-596.

[Gannett, W. C. and E. E. Hale.] "The Freedmen at Port Royal." *North American Review* 101 (July 1865): 1-28.

Higginson, T. W. "Negro Spirituals." *Atlantic Monthly* (June 1867): 685-694.

———. "Up the Edisto." *Atlantic Monthly* (August 1867): 157-165

Homer, Bigart. "Hunger in America." *New York Times*, February 16, 1969.

House, Grace Bigelow. "The Little Foe of All the World." *Southern Workman* 35 (November 1906): 598-614.

———. "The Penn School and the Farmers' Conference." *Southern Workman* 36 (January 1907): 58-60.

———. "Promise of Better Days." *Southern Workman* 37 (October 1908): 547-557.

———. "Stormy." *Southern Workman* 39 (April 1910): 221-233.

———. "The Fiftieth Anniversary of Penn School." *Southern Workman* 41 (May 1912): 316-320.

———. "The Need and Purpose of Industrial Education." *The Human Way: Addresses on Race Problems at the Southern Sociological Congress, Atlanta, 1913* Nashville, TN: Southern Sociological Congress, 1913.

——. "How Freedom Came to Big Pa." *Southern Workman* 45 (April 1916): 217-226.

——. "Roads of Learning on St. Helena." *Progressive Education* 4 (April 1937): 246-255.

——. "The Long Look." *Christian Endeavor World* (31 December 1944): 246-255.

Howard, Thomas D. "Before and After Emancipation." *Unitarian Review* (August 1888): 136-144.

James, Helen Lou. "Why the Penn School is Needed on St. Helena Island." *Southern Workman* 37 (February 1908): 90-94.

Kuyper, George A. "The Powerful Influence of a Notable School." *Southern Workman* 60 (January 1931): 29-32.

McKim, J. M. "Negro Songs," *Dwight's Journal of Music* 19 (August 9, 1862): 148-149.

McKim, Lucy. "Songs of the Port Royal Contrabands." *Dwight's Journal of Music* 21 (November 8, 1862): 254-255.

Marcel [F. W. Allen]. "The Negro Dialect." *Nation* 1 (December 14, 1865): 744-745.

Mitchell, Samuel C. "Industrial Education in the South." *Southern Workman* 39 (June 1910): 326-334.

——. "My Neighbor, The Negro." *Southern Workman* 40 (March 1911): 134-142.

——. "Signs of Growing Cooperation." *Southern Workman* 43 (October 1914): 552-559.

Murphy, Jeanette Robinson. "The Survival of African Music in America." *Popular Science Magazine* 55 (1899): 660-672.

Norris, Thaddeus. "Negro Superstitions." *Lippincott's Magazine* 6 (July 1870): 90-95.

Owens, William. "Folklore of the Southern Negro." *Lippincott's Magazine* 20 (December 1877): 748-755.

Peabody, Francis G. "Education for Life." *Southern Workman* 55 (June 1926): 248-256.

Pierce, Edward L. "The Freedmen at Port Royal." *Atlantic Monthly* 12 (September 1863): 293-315.

Raymond, Charles A. "Religious Life of the Negro Slave." *Harper's New Monthly Magazine* 27 (September 1863): 676-682.

Rowe, George C. "The Negroes of the Sea Islands." *Southern Workman* 29 (December 1900): 709-715.

Sage, E. C. "The Hampton Spirit." *Southern Workman* 46 (October 1917): 606.

Showers, Susan. "A Weddin' and a Buryin' in the Black Belt." *New England Magazine* 18 (1898): 478-483.

Spaulding, H. G. "Under the Palmetto." *Continental Monthly* 4 (1863): 188-203.

Stetson, George R. "The Negro's Need in Education." *Unitarian Review* (February 1887): 137-150.

Towne, Laura M. "Pioneer Work on the Sea Islands." *Southern Workman* 30 (July 1901): 396-401.

Unknown Author. "The Real Aim of Industrial Schools." *Southern Workman* 37 (January 1908): 374-375.

Unknown Author. "The South As It Is." *The Nation* 22 (November 30, 1865): 682-683.

Unknown Author. "Two Weeks at Port Royal." *Harper's New Monthly Magazine* 24 (1863): 110-118.

Unknown Author. "Slave Songs of the United States." *Lippincott's Magazine* 1 (March 1868): 341-343.

Unknown Author. "Songs of the Blacks" *Dwight's Journal of Music* 9 (November 15, 1856): 51-52.

Weatherford, W. D. "First Steps in Solving the Race Problem." *Southern Workman* 39 (November 1910): 589-592.

———. "Negro Training in the South." *Southern Workman* 41 (October 1912): 550-558.

———. "The Basis of Understanding Between the Races." *Southern Workman* 46 (December 1916): 655-661.

Williams, W. T. B. "The Yankee Schoolma'am in Negro Education." *Southern Education* 44 (February 1915): 73-80.

Wood, L. H. "A Negro Island Community." *New York Evening Post*, May 8, 1910.

Books

Billington, Ray Allen, editor. *The Journal of Charlotte L. Forten*. New York: W. W. Norton, 1981.

Botume, Elizabeth Hyde. *First Days Amongst the Contrabands*. Boston: Lee and Shephard Publishers, 1893.

Conroy, Pat. *The Water is Wide*. Boston: Houghton Mifflin, 1972.

Cooley, Rososa B. *Homes of the Freed*. New Republic, Inc., 1926.

———. *School Acres: An Adventure in Rural Education*. New Haven, CT: Yale University Press, 1930.

Higginson, Thomas Wentworth. *Army Life in a Black Regiment.* East Lensing: Michigan State University Press, 1960 (1870).

Holland, R. S., editor. *The Letters and Diaries of Laura M. Towne.* Cambridge, MA: Riverside Press, 1912.

Howard, O. O. *Letters from the South: Conditions of the Freedmen.* Washington, DC: Howard University Press, 1870.

Johnson, Clifton H., editor. *God Struck Me Dead: Religious Conversion Experiences and Autobiographies of Ex-Slaves.* Philadelphia: United Church Press, 1969.

Jones, T. J. *Negro Education: A Study of the Private and Higher Schools for Colored People in the United States.* Washington DC: Government Printing Office, 1917.

Livermore, Mary A. *My Story of the War.* Hartford, Conn.: A. D. Worthington and Company, 1891.

Loram, Charles T. *Adaptation of the Penn School Methods to Education in South Africa.* New York: Phelps-Stokes Fund, 1927.

Lyell, Charles. *A Second Visit to the United States.* New York: Harper & Brothers, Publishers, 1849.

Pearson, Elizabeth Ware, editor. *Letters from Port Royal, 1862-1868.* Boston: W. B. Clarke, 1906.

Taylor, Susan King. *Reminiscences of My Life in Camp.* Arno Press, Inc., 1968 (1902).

Weatherford, W. D. *Negro Life in the South.* New York: Association Press, 1911.

——. *Present Forces in Negro Progress.* New York: Association Press, 1912.

Woofter, Thomas Jackson. *Black Yeomanry: Life on St. Helena Island.* New York: Henry Holt and Company, 1930.

Secondary Resources

Articles

Baer, Hans A. "An Overview of Ritual, Oratory and Music in Southern Black Religion." *The Southern Quarterly* 23 (Spring 1985): 5-14.

Baird, Keith E. "Guy B. Johnson Revisited: Another Look at Gullah." *Journal of Black Studies* 10 (June 1980): 425-435.

Bascom, William R. "Acculturation Among the Gullah Negroes." *American Anthropologist* 43 (Jan-Mar 1941): 43-50.

Costen, Melva W. "Singing Praise to God in African American Worship Contexts." In *African American Religious Studies: An Interdisciplinary Anthology,* edited by Gayraud Wilmore. Durham, NC: Duke University Press, 1989.

Creel, Margaret Washington. "Gullah Attitudes Toward Life and Death." In *Africanisms in American Culture,* edited by Joseph E. Holloway. Bloomington: Indiana University Press, 1991.

Fulton, Richard M. "The Political Structure of Poro in Kpelle Society." *American Anthropologist* 74 (1972): 1218-1233.

Geertz, Clifford. "Religion as a Cultural System." In *Anthropological Approaches to the Study of Religion,* edited by Michael Banton. London: Routledge Press, 1968.

Glazier, Stephen D. "Mourning in the Afro-Baptist Tradition." *The Southern Quarterly* 23 (Spring 1985): 141-156.

Goldsmith, Peter. "Healing and Denominationalism on the Georgia Coast." *The Southern Quarterly* 23 (Spring 1985): 83-98.

Greene, Carroll, Jr. "Coming Home Again: Artist Johnathan Green Returns to His Gullah Roots." *American Visions* 5 (Feb 1990): 44-52.

Hazzard-Gordon, Katrina. "African-American Vernacular Dance." *Journal of Black Studies* 15 (June 1985): 427-445.

Herskovits, Melville J. "The Negro in the New World: The Statement of a Problem." *American Anthropologist* 32 (1930): 145-155.

Hoffman, Edwin D. "From Slavery to Self-Reliance." *Journal of Negro History* 41 (January 1956): 8-42.

Johnson, Charles S. "A Southern Negro's View of the South." *The Journal of Negro Education* 26 (Winter 1957): 4-9.

Jackson, Luther P. "The Educational Efforts of the Freedmen's Bureau and the Freedmen's Aid Societies in South Carolina, 1862-1872." *The Journal of Negro History* 8 (January 1923): 1-40

Jones-Jackson, Patricia. "Oral Tradition of Prayer in Gullah." *Journal of Religious Thought* 39 (Spring/Summer 1982):21-33.

Keister, Kim. "Island Haven." *Historic Preservation* (September 1994): 45-95.

Leavell, Ullin W. "Trends of Philanthropy in Negro Education: A Survey." *The Journal of Negro Education* 2 (January 1933): 38-52.

Leone, Mark P. and Parker B. Potter, Jr. "Introduction: Issues in Historical Archaeology." In *The Recovery of Meaning: Historical Archaeology in the Eastern United States*, edited by Mark P. Leone and Parker B. Potter, Jr., 1988, 1-22.

Little, K. L. "The Poro Society as an Arbiter of Culture." *African Studies* 7 (March 1948): 1-13.

——. "The Role of the Secret Society in Cultural Specialization." *American Anthropologist* 51 (Apr-June 1949): 199-212.

Long, Charles H. "Assessment and New Departures for a Study of Black Religion in the United States of America." *African American Religious Studies: An Interdisciplinary Anthology*, edited by Gayraud Wilmore. Durham, NC:

Duke University Press, 1989.

McPherson, James M. "White Liberals and Black Power in Negro Education, 1865-1915." *American Historical Review* 75 (June 1970): 1357-

Moore, Janie Gilliard. "Africanisms Among Blacks of the Sea Islands." *Journal of Black Studies* 10 (June 1980): 467-480.

Pease, William H. "Three Years Among the Freedmen: William C. Gannett and the Port Royal Experiment." *Journal of Negro History* 42 (April 1957): 98-117.

Pierson, Willaim D. "An African Background for American Negro Folktales?" *Journal of American Folklore* 84 (Apr-June 1971): 204-214.

Robbins, Gerald. "Rossa B. Cooley and the Penn School: Social Dynamo in a Negro Rural Subculture, 1901-1930." *The Journal of Negro Education* 33 (Winter 1964): 43-51.

Rosenfeld, Jeff. "The Forgotten Hurricane." *Weatherwise* 46 (August/September 1993): 13-18.

Saunders, William C. "Sea Islands Then and Now." *Journal of Black Studies* 10 (June 1980): 481-492.

Simpson, Robert. "The Shout and Shouting in Slave Religion of the United States." *The Southern Quarterly* 23 (Spring 1985): 34-46.

Smith, John P. "Cultural Preservation of the Sea Island Gullah: A Black Social Movement in the Post-Civil Rights Era." *Rural Sociology* 56, no.2 (1991): 284-298.

Smith, Therese. "Chanted Prayer in Southern Black Churches." *The Southern Quarterly* 23 (Spring 1985): 70-82.

Smith, Timothy. "Progressivism in American Education, 1880-1900." *Harvard Educational Review* 31 (Spring 1961): 168-193.

South, Stanley. "Santa Elena: Threshold of Conquest." In *The Recovery of Meaning: Historical Archaeology in the Eastern United States*, edited by Mark P. Leone and Parker B. Potter, Jr., 1988, 31f.

Spiro, Melford E. "Religion: Problems of Definition and Explanation." In *Anthropological Approaches to the Study of Religion*, edited by Michael Banton. London, 1966.

Starks, George L. Jr. "Singing 'Bout a Good Time: Sea Island Religious Music." *Journal of Black Studies* 10 (June 1980): 437-444.

Szwed, John F. "Africa Lies Just Off Georgia." *Africa Report* 15 (October 1970): 29-31.

Twining, Mary Arnold. "Movement and Dance on the Sea Islands." *Journal of Black Studies* 15 (June 1985): 463-479.

———. "Sources in the Folklore and Folklife of the Sea Islands." *Southern Folklore Quarterly* 39 (1975): 135-150.

Twining, Mary A. and Keith E. Baird. "The Significance of Sea Island Culture." *Journal of Black Studies* 10:4 (June 1980): 379-386.

———. "Introduction to Sea Island Folklife." *Journal of Black Studies* 10 (June 1980): 387-416.

Unknown Author. "A Social Experiment: The Port Royal Journal of Charlotte L. Forten, 1862-1863." *The Journal of Negro History* 35 (July 1950): 233-263.

Washington, Joseph R. "Folk Religion and Negro Congregations: The Fifth Religion." In *African American Religious Studies: An Interdisciplinary Anthology*, edited by Gayraud Wilmore. Durham, NC: Duke University Press, 1989.

Wheaton, Thomas R. and Patrick H. Garrow. "Acculturation and the Archaeological Record in the Carolina Lowcountry." In *The Archaeology of Slavery and Plantation Life*, edited by Theresa A. Singleton. New York: Academic Press, 1985.

Books

Boys, Mary. *Educating in Faith*. Chicago: Sheed and Ward, 1993.

Creel, Margaret Washington. *A Peculiar People: Slave Religion and Community Culture Among the Gullahs*. New York: New York University Press, 1988.

Cremin, Lawrence A. *The Transformation of the School: Progressivism in American Education, 1876-1957*. New York: Alfred A. Knopf, 1961.

Crum, Mason. *Gullah: Negro Life in the Carolina Sea Islands*. Durham, NC: Duke University Press, 1965 (1940).

Douglas, Mary, editor. *Implicit Meanings*. London: Henley and Boston, 1975.

Jacoway, Elizabeth. *Yankee Missionaries in the South: The Penn School Experiment*. Baton Rouge: Louisiana State University, 1980.

Jones-Jackson, Patricia. *When Roots Die: Endangered Traditions on the Sea Islands*. Athens: University of Georgia Press, 1987.

Johnson, Guion Griffis. *A Social History of the Sea Islands*. Chapel Hill: University of North Carolina Press, 1930.

Mbiti, John S. *New Testament Eschatology in an African Background*. NY Oxford University Press, 1971.

———. *Introduction to African Religion*. Portsmouth, NH: Heinemann Educational Books, 1991.

Parsons, Elsie Clews. *Folk-Lore of the Sea Islands, South Carolina*. New York: American Folklore Society, 1923.

McPherson, James M. *The Abolitionist Legacy From Reconstruction to the NAACP*. Princeton NJ: Princeton University Press, 1976.

Pickering, W.S.F., editor. *Durkheim on Religion*. Boston: Routledge and Kegan Paul, 1975.

Puckett, N. N. *Folk Beliefs of the Southern Negro*. Chapel Hill: University of North Carolina Press, 1926.

Raboteau, Albert J. *Slave Religion*. New York: Oxford University Press, 1978.

Rose, Willie Lee. *Rehearsal For Reconstruction: The Port Royal Experiment*. New York: The Bobbs-Merrill Company, Inc., 1964.

Stuckey, Sterling. *Slave Culture: Nationalist Theory and the Foundations of Black America*. New York: Oxford University Press, 1987.

Whiten, N. E., Jr. and J. F. Szwed, editors. *Afro-American Anthropology, Contemporary Perspectives*. New York: Free Press, 1970.

Wood, Peter H. *Black Majority*. New York: W. W. Norton & Company, 1974.

Woofter, Thomas Jackson. *Teaching in Rural Schools*. New York: Houghton Mifflin [1917].

Unpublished Dissertations

Burns, Betsy Jacoway. "The Penn School, 1862-1948: A Look at Negro Education in South Carolina." Ph.D. diss., University of North Carolina, 1968.

Doe, Kenneth C. "The Praise House Tradition and Community Renewal at St. Joseph Baptist Church." D. Min. thesis, Erskine Theological Seminary, 1991.

Guthrie, Patricia. "Catch Sense: The Meaning of Plantation Membership on St. Helena Island, S. C." Ph.D. diss., University of Rochester, 1977.

Jackson, Patricia Ann Jones. "The Status of Gullah: An Investigation of Convergent Processes." Ph.D. diss., University of Michigan, 1978.

Jordon, Francis Harold. "Across the Bridge: Penn School and Penn Center." Ed.D. diss., University of South Carolina, 1991.

Lawton, Samuel Miller. "The Religious Life of South Carolina Coastal and Sea Island Negroes." Ph.D. diss., Peabody College for Teachers, 1939.

Luker, Ralph Edwin. "The Northern Social Gospel Prophets and the Negro: 1890-1917." Ph.D. diss., University of North Carolina, 1969.

Oldendorf, Sandra Brenneman, "Highlander Folk School and the South Carolina Sea Island Citizenship Schools." Ed.D. dissertation, University of Kentucky, 1987.

Smedley, Katherine. "The Northern Teacher on the South Carolina Sea Islands." M.A. thesis, University of North Carolina, 1932.

Twining, Mary Arnold. "An Examination of African Retentions in the Folk Culture of the South Carolina and Georgia Sea Islands." Ph.D. diss., Indiana University, 1977.

Watkins, June T. "Strategies of Social Control in an Isolated Community: The Case of the Gullah of South Carolina's St. Helena Island." Ph.D. diss., Indiana University of Pennsylvania, 1993.

Index